PLAYSCRIPT 105

THE NUMBER OF THE BEAST
and
Flaming Bodies

Snoo Wilson

JOHN CALDER : LONDON
RIVERRUN PRESS : NEW YORK

First published in Great Britain in 1983 by
John Calder (Publishers) Limited
18 Brewer Street, London W1R 4AS

First published in the USA in 1983 by
Riverrun Press Inc
175 Fifth Avenue, New York, NY 10010

All performing rights are strictly reserved and applications for
performance should be made in writing to Jenne Casarotto,
Douglas Rae, 28 Charing Cross Road, London WC2. No
performance may be given unless a licence has been obtained
prior to rehearsal.

British Library Cataloguing in Publication Data
Wilson, Snoo
    The Number of the Beast, and, Flaming Bodies
—(Playscript series; 105)
I. Title   II. Series
822'.914   PR6073.I/

ISBN 0-7145-3959-7

SUBSIDISED BY THE
Arts Council
OF GREAT BRITAIN

Typeset in 10/11 Times by Gilbert Composing Services
Printed and bound in Great Britain by
Hillman Printers (Frome) Ltd.

CONTENTS

INTRODUCTION

The Beast was written originally for the Royal Shakespeare Company, and was then a vast sprawling and ambitious play which attempted to account for all the significant background influences on Crowley. His family upbringing in the Plymouth Brethren, a sect of strict and teetotal non-Conformists, with a father who (bizarrely) made money out of beer, was a lay preacher and died of cancer: his sexual initiation, and at the latter end of his life, his removal to a kind of ghostly historical limbo in the company of Frank Harris.

Productions of this version chewed heartily on the subject matter without being able to swallow it. Finally the last indignity was a disgraceful pirated musical version which decided me to write the piece. If anyone was going to tinker with it, it would be me. I set about rewriting it with the help of the New York Theatre Studio, who provided actors' workshops and readings of the play to this end, and so they bear a considerable credit for the play in its present form.

Having left history to look after itself, it was relatively easy to write a play about the man. I am not a social historian and so was pleased to leave social accountability out of the story. Crowley is by most accounts outside The Pale, and there was not much point in trying to explain to people how he got there, if the effort obscured the celebration of his attempt.

In the first act, Crowley's child dies and the fabric of his commune synchronisticly unwinds. In the second act, forced to return to England, he meets a magical opponent of a status which provokes first demonstrations, then envy and disbelief, and finally the separation of Crowley from his sexual alter ego, his Scarlet Woman.

Gerald Yorke, who knew Crowley well without being unduly awed or repulsed by him, described him as a 'false Messiah'. His falsity was very much a part of his time. He was in the Order of the Golden Dawn, a magical order, in London at the same time as W.B. Yeats, but could never decide whether he was poet, magician, hoaxer or gentleman. When one failed he fell back on the other. Like many discontinous characters, it is difficult to know how seriously 'Old Crow' took his messianic duties. The Book Of The Law lay abandoned in a trunk for years before Crowley decided to take this piece of automatic writing and make it the bible, as it were, of the New Age. When Crowley and Yeats met in the Order's temple in the Fulham Road, the other social revolutionaries were meeting off the Tottenham Court Road in equally unpromising circumstances. Whatever one thinks of the effects of the cult of materialism, in the days of the Golden Dawn, its prophets were as reedy and outnumbered as the table-turners, so I feel one should be ready to forgive the latter their enormous ambitions, for the world; they are simply very much of their time.

Crowley was in fact demonstrating the guru's maddening indifference to worldly acclamation *before* he had enough of it for the attitude to count for much. Unfortunately for him there was also an explosion of print in the form of cheap popular newspapers. Crowley's subsequent career was blighted by his inability to deal with this. The Messiah never managed to turn the fact that Sex Magick made a good headline to his advantage. As is often the case, it never got much beyond being a headline, and the more provocative, learned and religious nature of Crowley's quest got hinted to death, as it were, in the press.

Crowley was not only a practical joker at his own expense, but also a man of considerable intellect who could have been a poet of some stature if he'd had the patience. His career into the 'unconscious' is a voyage taken at roughly the same time as those other giants of inner space, Freud and Jung. While the latter two started as doctors and painstakingly staked out the 'new' area of psychology as their preserve, Crowley was less responsible. He failed to institutionalise himself properly and neglected the essential nurturing of powerful and wealthy helpers who would help him get the New Aeon on the road. Crowley honeymooned in Cheops chamber of the Pyramids, to write The Book Of The Law. Freud went to Paris to study the demonstrations of the great Charcot with hysterical patients, and caught the pithy aside that their problems were 'toujours la chose genitale'. Freud's translation of this into a potent mythology comes with all the trappings of science. His 'scientific' enquiries into the mind are 'scientific' in order to erect a temple of orthodoxy, with the penis at its centre. Only Jung was brave enough to flout this, and wadded into the boggy swamps of magic, astrology, synchronicity, to come up with questions which suggest answers richer and stranger than anything even Crowley was after.

I have allowed Crowley two small magical effects. Concievably, they could be hypnotically induced on the subjects in the play, but I have written them as absolutes, though they should rise smoothly out of the text. I have done this partly to show that magic in the play is like any other kind of reality, a contract between interested parties, and partly as a slight tipping of the hat towards Old Crow, or his shade, who elsewhere in the play I have constrained, without asking, to dance for me.

Flaming Bodies is about a fat girl with agoraphobia who is stuck on the top floor of a skyscraper building in Los Angeles. To live is to fall and she is afraid to descend. In the play I have obliged her to see an aeroplane accident over Ankara, of a particularly horrific kind. It actually took place: one plane tore a passenger plane open over the city and many passengers were tipped out in mid-air. I may have invented the fact that some of the passengers were on fire as they fell, in order to make it a 'better' story and to fit the title, but my own connection with the accident was through a witness who I met four years afterwards: the accident was one about which I had had a premonition strong enough to remember after four years, although nothing else has occurred to link me with the crash beyond my meeting a man who saw it, and on whom it made not unnaturally a strong impression.

Mercedes Mordecai has been fired from her job but continues to haunt the office. The play is about her fears overnight and her accumulation of enough knowledge and self confidence to be able to leave in the morning, even though no externals have changed. In the play, she is obsessed by a story which she has been touting for a film of a female Christ. She is convinced her boss has stolen it. Her nightmares are shot through with the story of her as the suffering hub of the universe.

What happens in the bulk of the play is her dream. She falls asleep and we follow her into her dream life. She is alone. But the end to the character's solitude must happen in order for progress to be made. A car comes through the window of the thirty second floor.

The designer and stage crew did us proud, in the end. But the commissioning theatre was initially fretful and puzzled about the problems of a car bursting into a boxset. Correctly supposing that this concern over technical problem demonstrated a failure to become involved with the script on a passionate, artistic level, I offered the play to the ICA theatre, who put it on, and it was extremely popular. People even queued for returns; it was known as 'the play where the car comes through the window'. I was delighted to have given birth to a play which people liked so much, but the car is a flaming red herring. It marks the beginning of the descent into the Abyss, the unconscious, out of which the main character slowly pieces together the clues that this *is* a dream world, and thereby manages to escape to daylight.

In defence of writing a dream, I would like to say this. I suspect that our ancestors who laid down the foundations of our present brains and nervous sytems may, in the protozoic ooze, have collected and passed down to us a much more careless idea of sequence and understanding than our cognitive, minute-stricken conscious minds know about, and that we are not only playing to ourselves in present time, but to the gallery where sit our ancestors. And they don't quite understand theatre. Theatre is half folly, and having not invented reason yet, they would have no cause to call upon folly, its opposite. And I suspect that theatre can be an engagement with these monsters within ourselves, though we can never entirely tame them. We are offering sops to Dionysus.

SNOO WILSON

The Number of the Beast was first performed at the Bush Theatre,
London on 4 February 1982. The cast was:

ALEISTER CROWLEY	John Stride
MME POITIER	Maxine Audley
PETERS	Eric Roy Evans
URFF, DIDEROT	Matthew Guinness
NUTTALL	Colin Higgins
RANDY	Steven Mackintosh
GLORIA	Michelle Newell

Directed by Robin Lefèvre

Designed by John Byrne

The play may be doubled for eight characters as follows:

Act One	*Act Two*
CROWLEY	CROWLEY
LARIA	LARIA
PETERS	MAITRE d'HÔTEL
URFF	DIDEROT
NUTTALL	YEATS
GLORIA	MAUD GONNE
NORA	MME POITIER
RANDY	

The Number of the Beast

CROWLEY *alone. Dusk. Dawn chorus. A figure emerges out of the shadows. Hat, wig, black coat, American.*

CROWLEY. Is that Laria?
PETERS. No.
CROWLEY. Nuttall?
PETERS. Er no, I'm not Nuttall.
CROWLEY. Urff?
PETERS. No.
CROWLEY. Well you must be a burglar. Have a chair. Come from Cefalu?
PETERS. I walked through the night.
CROWLEY. Want to discover your true will?
PETERS. Er—yes—I do.
CROWLEY. Good. Go and stand in the shrubbery, over there, and watch the sunrise with your back to Cefalu. Follow the sun's course through the sky and when it is completely dark, come back to the abbey.
PETERS. Alright.

Exits. The growing light discovers the set, the patio of a broken-down Sicilian farmhouse. Enter GLORIA, *from within.*

GLORIA. I can't sleep. Bloody birds.
CROWLEY. That **word**, Gloria, that **word**.
GLORIA. Oh sorry.
CROWLEY. Who?
GLORIA. *One* is sorry.
CROWLEY. Ruthless self-criticism is the only thing that will ever free you. The I is not free to criticize. The I is trapped in a world of want.
GLORIA. One didn't realise. *(Brightly)* I'll get the razor and cut my arm once for every time—how many times is it?
CROWLEY. A wise riddle to ask the cosmic egg.
GLORIA. I've forgotten.
CROWLEY. That's one more, to what you forgot. Infinity plus one.
GLORIA. Sorry.

CROWLEY. Don't be sorry! Listen to my godlike conversation.

GLORIA. I'll get the razor.

CROWLEY. I. You're punishing yourself to please me. That's not the way.

GLORIA. I'm not.

CROWLEY. Again.

GLORIA. I think you're cruel.

CROWLEY. Your body is your bank. You should be prudent with your withdrawals. (GLORIA *is about to exit, but turns.*)

GLORIA. I don't want to do it!

CROWLEY. Quite right, in that there shall be no trade in human flesh. But secretly, you're hoarding. You delay the treatment and the disease only inconveniences you and your friends. You should come to the cure as one goes to a good restaurant, ready to meet the experience with a cheque.

GLORIA. I like my body. I like to give it to you—I don't want to cut it around—

CROWLEY. I . . . I . . . I.

GLORIA. Fuck you. Fuck the whole Abbey of Thelema.

CROWLEY. Impossible to pay the Abbey at Cefalu a greater compliment. What you say, against your own will, is may the Abbey prosper. Blaspheme all we need! The world is turned upside down! We're a pitiful minority! But we're the only people who exist. The rest of the human race, cut off from their subconscious, are nothing but a pack of cards.

GLORIA. You wrote to Trotsky, after the revolution.

CROWLEY. Yes I did write to Trotsky. He didn't reply. For three years after the revolution, Russia was alight with the flame of courage that could have swept the world like a prairie fire. But it went out. (LARIA *arrives.* GLORIA *goes.* CROWLEY *moves sofa, sits down and starts sniffing ether.* LARIA *watches him.*) It's getting brighter. Is that me, or the sun?

LARIA. Where've I been?

CROWLEY. As one incarnation said to another.

LARIA. What did you give me?

CROWLEY. Tiny dose of heroin. Harmless.

LARIA. Is it the sun or the moon?

CROWLEY. Excellent! Marvellous! The self-displaced! Your big ugly mouth does it again! Out of the mouths of babes, sucklings, and the Ape of Thoth.

LARIA. Oh Beast . . . I feel awful.

CROWLEY. What you said **shows** we are right to continue in what we are going. The moon displaces the sun. The first step to freeing the imagination from the dull pedantry of the solar system.

LARIA. Will I live?

CROWLEY. I!

4

LARIA. I'm too ill to lose blood slashing myself every time I say I. *(Curls up to him on the sofa)* Souls not stuck to the body! One drop more out—and away I go. Dead soul.

CROWLEY *(busy sniffing)*. What do you care?

LARIA. I don't mind dying here. I'd rather be here than where I came from.

CROWLEY. My scarlet woman.

LARIA. Beast. *(Pause)* Old Prick.

CROWLEY. No more or less.

LARIA. Beast. Get rid of Gloria.

CROWLEY. The Green Eyed Monster that doth mock . . .

LARIA. She doesn't fit in—

CROWLEY. The meat it feeds on. Why? *(Pause)*

LARIA. Suppose she's a spy from the Sunday Express. Or John Bull.

CROWLEY. In that case, she will have discovered that contrary to to popular belief the Beast 666 does not have a forked prick, from repeated mutual worship and inspection.

LARIA. **Spying.**

CROWLEY. Horatio Bottomley leering from between the cheeks of her arse. *(They both laugh fitfully)* Now there's a worthwhile prison for that man. *(Offers ether)* A snort?

LARIA. Why don't you get addicted?

CROWLEY. Character.

LARIA. Where's Satan?

CROWLEY. The dog died when you were ill.

LARIA. What?

CROWLEY. He went off in the hills.

LARIA. How long has he been gone?

CROWLEY. Week . . . two . . . I'd have to look at the diary. He may have been poisoned.

LARIA. Oh no!

CROWLEY. The last time the police came, they heard you call him.

LARIA. He didn't bite them. I was calling him off!

CROWLEY. Yes but they think that a dog called Satan in an incarnation.

LARIA. What's wrong with that?

CROWLEY. Nothing to us, but if you associate Satan with all the unrecognized elements in the unconscious mind, then you've got a dog with a poor reputation. How's Binky this morning? What's she doing?

LARIA. She's asleep. *(*CROWLEY *digs the I Ching out of a corner of the sofa)*

CROWLEY. D'you have any coins? I want to ask the I Ching what she's up for. Life, or . . . I can't do it the other way because little Randy set fire to the yarrow stalks.

LARIA. Oh. The little bastard.

CROWLEY. It was his will.

LARIA. He can't work miracles. He didn't set fire to them with his will!

CROWLEY. No, no, he is an imaginative child. He used a box of matches. Do what thou wilt shall be the whole of the law.

LARIA. Did you speak to Gloria about it? It's her child. *(CROWLEY shrugs)* He already says he's going to kill you and be the beast instead.

CROWLEY. Well we needn't worry for the moment, because his will is very small. *(NUTTALL appears completely naked. Genteel Midland accent, gangly, spectacles)*

NUTALL. Do what thou wilt shall be the only law.

CROWLEY & LARIA *(without looking up).* Love is the law, love under will.

CROWLEY. D'you have any small change about you, Nutall?

NUTTALL. Not at this moment. I'm going swimming.

CROWLEY. We're quite without currency and so unable to converse with the I Ching.

NUTTALL. I believe I have a threepenny bit in my waistcoat.

CROWLEY. We need three.

NUTTALL. I shall have to go and get it, you see because at the moment I don't have my waistcoat on. In face if you look you will see that I don't have anything on at all. I've thrown away all my inhibitions this morning, Frater Perdurabo, and just now me and Gloria performed an act of sex magic.

CROWLEY *(refuses to be impressed).* With what object in view?

NUTTALL. We were so carried away with the vital current that I lost sight of the object although she tells me she didn't. The object was to recover the dog, Satan, which I understand disappeared a few days before I arrived.

CROWLEY. What was the orgasm like?

NUTTALL. Well it would have been very good, I predict, as good as on Saturday, but little Randy came into the kitchen and threw pepper all over us.

CROWLEY. Did he leave any for breakfast?

NUTTALL. I don't know. I'll just go and rummage about in my pockets and see if I can get you a few coins. *(he goes out)*

CROWLEY. I really must say. Here we are, threatened with expulsion by the government through the English press, so poor we can't even remain in tune with the unconscious. Half the Abbey members weak with exhaustion from using their bodies as vehicles for their wills, and all they can think to ask about is the dog!

LARIA *(hostile).* What about Binky? Isn't that something wrong as well?

CROWLEY. If it is her will to die, then she will. Look at her progressed horoscope. She doesn't hang on by much.

LARIA. She wants to live.

CROWLEY. Who'd live for crying, and Allinson's gripe water?

LARIA. She had some watered wine yesterday. But she spent all her energy in this frenzy — can't we get Nuttall to get some money from his parents —

CROWLEY. By all means. I already have.

LARIA. Your daughter's dying, and we don't even know what's wrong with her!

CROWLEY. I'm a psychologist really. I can find out what's wrong with people's soul, because I go to their essence—but the body's more difficult. She has a will, to die. She puts her face to the wall— in the great scheme of things, it's nothing, but one's daughter—it's a bit hard. *(He is upset. Recovers.)* No more ego. No more self. Just the will. The current of the guardian angel is all one needs to listen to. We've had our spiritual crises. Now, it's plain sailing for the Logos of the Aeon and his scarlet woman. *(He sees NORA entering.)* Don't look up. It's the paranoid we sent to Coventry, up to spread her morning bile.

NUTTALL *comes back in with trousers.* NORA HENESSEY *comes in by other door. Harris tweed skirt, etc. Nobody looks at her.*

NORA. I know what you think of me. You have not forgotten me. You are all continually talking about me. Tearing my reputation to shreds. Sneering at my poetry—my paintings. You can't go on ignoring real talent, real genius. There's not one of you has any real artistic talent. Not one. The paintings of goats and semen in your rooms are childish pornography. How many of you know what the light is like in the morning on a blade of corn? You don't. You poison your bodies, and you poison your minds against me. But I don't hate you. In fact, I still regard you all as people who might have done something wonderful, but you have turned away from the light. Adultery and grave robbing kills even artists. Dante Gabriel Rossetti died a fat addict at sixty, because his hedonism, his excitement over decay and the macabre ruined his genius. I will not eat cakes of light. They are made of goat dung! You drag your followers down in the mud behind you. You have forbidden them to mention my name and so forth. What power do I have to destroy your fantastic persecution? I know. You know. It's called sanity. You've got to start somewhere. Here are some nut cutlets. This is your last chance. If you eat them today, then I will know that I am welcome. *(Puts them on the table.)* I shall go and spend the day watching the colours change on the sea. I don't want to come back and find them rolled in the dirt, or that the dog's eaten them. They're for you, all of you. I did it because I think you are sick, and you need help. A healthy society wouldn't have to forbid you to look at me, to mention my name! What have I done except declined advances to my body? If you like, that is my will, that I can't do the things which lead to your freedom. But I still exist, don't I?

I've put the little offering on the table. Have a good day.

CROWLEY. Don't touch them anyone. Don't mention that she's been. The ban on discussing her stands. That way, she knows that accusations of gossip are false and malicious. *(She exits.)*

NUTTALL. Three threepenny bits. *(He gives them.)*

CROWLEY. The first one, Nuttall, signifies the disappearance of your pains in the head, the second silences the mysterious voices leading you round Cambridge Circus, and the third opens your puny ego to the flood gates of the unconscious so that the self drowns. *(*NUTTALL *is overcome.)*

NUTTALL *(perturbed).* I don't think I will go to the beach after all. I feel perturbed by this knowledge. I think I ought to go and lie down.

CROWLEY. Practise a magical act by yourself, imagine yourself taken by Pan.

NUTTALL. Alright, anything you say.

CROWLEY. You have a disease. It's called the ego. That's why you get voices. Voices. Voices. . .

NUTTALL. But . . . the last time you said you heard them too.

CROWLEY. If you don't do what your will indicates, then you will get them back. **Voices**. . .

NUTTALL. Is there anything else I could do, not a magical act?

CROWLEY. Squeeze money from somewhere. How much money is your father sending?

NUTTALL. A hundred—but I'll give it to you when it arrives.

CROWLEY. Wire him to double it.

NUTTALL. It's a lot of money.

CROWLEY. What have you appointed me to instruct you in?

NUTTALL. The discovery of the unconscious.

CROWELY. Silence for a week, fast for two days, and the word 'I' is forbidden on pain of razor.

NUTTALL. When should I begin?

CROWLEY. When it feels right for you. Do things one at a time. If you wire your father, don't feel you have to bathe.

NUTTALL. Oh. Good. *(He leaves.)*

CROWLEY *(shaking coins).* With the lira inflating at the present rate, the longer we leave it, the more we get for our money later on. Invest in Cefalu, you copper bottomed capitalists! Save it all from the coming smash!

LARIA. Is there going to be a smash?

CROWLEY. Oh yes.

GLORIA *comes in with two buckets. One full of water and the other of clay.*

GLORIA. Your child is crying again.

CROWLEY. What did you do?

GLORIA. Came out and told its parents. *(*LARIA *runs off.)*

8

CROWLEY. Did you know that jealously destroy's magic, just as fast
    as hypocrisy or greed?
GLORIA. It's only natural. *(Pause. CROWLEY throws coins.*
    GLORIA makes pot.)
CROWLEY *(finishes doing the I ching).* Hexagram twenty three. . .
    oh.
GLORIA. What's the judgement?
CROWLEY. The judgement is 'Splitting apart. It does not further one
    to go anywhere.'
GLORIA. What's the image?
CROWLEY. 'The mountain rests upon the earth. The image of
    splitting apart. Thus those above can only ensure their decision by
    giving generously to those below.'
GLORIA. Any lines?
CROWLEY. Nothing else. That's it.
GLORIA. Somebody's going to leave.
CROWLEY. I'd like to think it applied to Nora Hennessey leaving the
    Abbey, rather than Binky leaving life. But whichever it means, it
    advises submitting to the bad time and staying quiet.
GLORIA. You'd better take its advice.
CROWLEY. 'It does not further one to go anywhere.' *(stands)* We'll
    have to do it here.
GLORIA. Do what?
CROWLEY. Carve a hole in the future. Right here.
GLORIA. But it says—
CROWLEY. Take my **body**. Consecrate with yours! Now! As you took
    Nuttall to pray for the dog. The duty we have lies with ourselves.
    Fay ce que vouldras. The world is ours only to discover our true will.
    Let's perform.
GLORIA. We didn't finish with the dog.
CROWLEY. Alright for the dog. And money in the post. And Binky.
GLORIA. Not Binky, not money.
CROWLEY. The world is alive with channels and currents and some
    of them run with gold.
GLORIA. I only want to do the dog.
CROWLEY. The dog then. *(Advances)* Smell me. I'll eat you. I'll make
    lunar cakes of the skin from your· breasts and menstrual blood, and
    we'll find Satan for a start. You don't have to do Binky right away.
    Wait till it feels right for you. Smell me. *(She does reluctantly.)*
    And is it this anointed body that you shall touch.
GLORIA. It is.
CROWLEY. You dog whore. You dog faced bitch titted snarl jowled
    dog. Bitch in the manger. *(GLORIA is enjoying this.)* Bitch. Bitch.
    (GLORIA closes her eyes.)
GLORIA. Do the dog, do the dog, Satan, Satan . . . *(They stand,*
    close but not touching.) I can feel Satan's body . . . his claws, his hot
    breath . . . bush tail and a big, red cock . . . I wanted to take the

cock and the glory of Horus and the great work—shove it in
the flames of fornication.

CROWLEY. Show it. Love that dog. Bring him close. Don't let
him go.

GLORIA. Love it.

CROWLEY. A dog. A magical dog.

GLORIA. Where are you? Come back . . . Sweet doggie . . .
sweet doggie . . .

CROWLEY. Good, very good, now later on at the moment of
orgasm I want you to concentrate on Binky—*(They open
their eyes.)*

GLORIA. It's no good. I don't love him. I love the dog. Sorry.

CROWLEY *goes back and lies on sofa. Defeated. Puts hat over eyes.*
NUTTALL *comes back.*

NUTTALL. Er. Frater Perdurabo. I was lying on my bed in a
fever of discovery of your explanation of the relationship of the
unconscious to the conscious.

CROWLEY. Before you start—have you wired your father yet?
For the three hundred pounds—Four hundred pounds?

NUTTALL. I would like to thank you—

CROWLEY. Are you deaf too?

NUTTALL. What?

CROWLEY. **Are you deaf too?**

NUTTALL. Er no—

CROWLEY *(fast)*. I asked you about your father.

NUTTALL. Er—

CROWLEY. What?

NUTTALL. No.

CROWLEY. What?

NUTTALL *(quickly)*. No I didn't.

CROWLEY. Little flurry of words. What were they again?

NUTTALL *(courage)*. **No I didn't.** *(Pause)* I didn't mean to shout.

CROWLEY. You didn't mean to **what?**

NUTTALL. Shout! But I will soon, send for the money.

CROWLEY. The last bit?

NUTTALL. Which?

CROWLEY. The bit about the money.

NUTTALL. Soon.

CROWLEY *(magnanimous)*. There's no hurry.

NUTTALL. I'll do it before lunch. I just wanted to thank you for
your help.

CROWLEY. Not at all. It's practically involuntary. Sheer musings
aloud on the human condition. But Nuttall you must be
prepared for—very soon—this whole situation to precipitate
itself in a spiritual crisis. I could create money, but what's the
point of behaving like the treasury? This is going to be a test

10

of your faith.

NUTTALL. My father's a stern man.

CROWLEY. Precisely.

NUTTALL. I'll have to grovel and tell him lies.

CROWLEY. If you are true to yourself, you will find that you hate your father.

NUTTALL. I sometimes wish him dead. Yes.

CROWLEY. Lying to him should be a pleasure then. Tell him you broke **three** legs.

NUTTALL. Oh he'd never accept that—

CROWLEY. Wasn't your third leg permanently dégonflé when you came here? And hasn't it been put together well? I mean it's worked on absolutely everybody. It's a distaff! A broomhandle! A pillar of the Great Work! You, not money, are the centre of all creation!

NUTTALL. I'll tell him. Something else. Maybe. . . something expensive, I don't know.

CROWLEY. Good man.

NUTTALL. This instant.

CROWLEY. Love and do what thou wilt.

NUTTALL. I do this out of love for you, and Gloria, and Laria and Binky—and little Randy and love is the will, love under law. *(Exits.)*

CROWLEY. I must be the greatest psychologist in the world. I **can** cure people if they allow it. The next religion after Crowleyanity's going to be a poser. I mean, when the many are reduced to one, to what is the one reduced? *(Lies down. GLORIA makes pot. CROWLEY starts up.)* Footsteps? Did I hear footsteps?

GLORIA. No. *(RANDY comes in silently with the mail, behind.)* The mail's come.

CROWLEY *(interest).* The post! There must be about six weeks worth there. A block on Mercury, the winged messenger has gone, as predicted. Here. *(RANDY doesn't move.)* Bring it here, Randy. *(RANDY doesn't move.)* Alright, give it first to your mother, and then to Uncle Alick.

RANDY. Beast.

CROWLEY. Alright, Uncle Beast.

RANDY. Beast 666.

CROWLEY. Uncle Beast 666. *(warmly)* The wickedest man in the world. . .

RANDY. Beast.

CROWLEY. Come on, Randy, you've got the future of our whole world in your hands. Don't be shy of it. Put it in piles, one for each person. *(Pause)*

RANDY *(villainous).* Sssss

CROWLEY. Here. *(RANDY drops a couple of letters and retreats, his arms full, eyes still on CROWLEY. LARIA comes in. CROWLEY passes the letters to her.)* From your mother.

The ADULTS *stand in a menacing ring round* RANDY.

GLORIA. Randy. Come to mother.

CROWLEY. We're all equal here, you don't have to give them to your mother if you don't want. We're all your mother. Come to mother. Just divide them up.

LARIA. Thank you for my two Randy, they are very nice and welcome. Could I have some more addressed to me?

RANDY *is concerned against the audience. He starts to tear the mail up. They all grab for him and stop him halfway.*

RANDY. I am the Beast! I am the Beast!

CROWLEY. No, I am!

RANDY. I shall be the Beast, I shall be—spear you with my evil eye—and make you listen to me and what I say—I'll turn you into pissy toads.

GLORIA. Randy—

RANDY. Pissy toads. And I'll stick a straw in you and blow you up till you burst. Pus.

GLORIA. Not your mother, you won't.

RANDY. Yes I will. I am the Beast! You're a shitbag. You made me. I am the Beast etc. etc. *(Flees off out of their clutches, exits.)*

LARIA. Can't you control him?

GLORIA *(protective)*. You shouldn't ask him to do things he can't do! It upsets him!

LARIA *(having got most of mail)*. Fascinating.

GLORIA. You shouldn't ask him to do things he can't do!

LARIA. Like stop himself from setting fire to everything!

GLORIA. Beast shouldn't have asked him *(voice quavery with protectiveness)* to parcel the letters out—so aggressively. *(Pause)* He can't read. *(Pause.)*

CROWLEY *(ironic)*. Oh, excellent.

GLORIA. It's like asking a cripple to dance.

LARIA. He could learn!

GLORIA. He is slow. Where are the schools here?

LARIA. Nobody's ever tried to teach him.

CROWLEY. And why should they? I think he's a very interesting specimen as it is.

GLORIA. He's my son!

CROWLEY. What does it matter? He's the child of everyone here.

GLORIA. He's my son! I had him before I came, and I'm going to take him away with me.

CROWLEY. Is he going to learn to read before you leave? *(Pause.)*

12

LARIA. He's uncontrollable.

GLORIA. He's overtired.

LARIA. So are we!

CROWLEY. Ah. Here's a letter to Urff, addressed to 'The One Eyed Worm, Cefalu, Sicily.' *(CROWLEY opens packages.)*

LARIA. What's that?

CROWLEY. Papers, You can have it. *(He gives them to her, uninterested.)*

LARIA opens paper. Sunday Express. Headline,|AT ALEISTER CROWLEY'S UNSPEAKABLE ORGY. DRUG FIEND EXPOSED. DISGUSTING RITES. Another—John Bull.

LARIA *(reads)*. 'Disgusting black magician practises|foul rites with numerous women. Exclusive interview.' INTERVIEW! Joanna Hammett. . . the traitoress! . . . She was only here for lunch! 'The ex-debutante closed her eyes and went pale. I cannot describe it.' She's as much of a deb as my arse is!

CROWLEY. They make them up. They didn't get an interview.

LARIA. Well, they described her jewellery right. Pendant green stone—'Crowley fixed me with his hypnotic gaze and said, I am the wickedest man in the world. I sacrifice children. I like their blood.'

GLORIA. Do they mean that about Binky?

CROWLEY *(wearily)*. No.

LARIA. There's a description of the Abbey. 'A low farmhouse without sanitation. The bushes or the sea are used for toilet purposes. . . ' *(CROWLEY deigns to look.)*

CROWLEY. They've got all the colours wrong. Blue for brown— brown for red. So magically it cannot harm us.

LARIA. 'Goats are used. Bodily functions are openly talked about and foul rites practised every night with cockerels. The police are keeping an eye on the situation, and the British Consulate has been urged to expel these loathsome practices from the fair shores of Sicily before they sully the name of Albion further.'

CROWLEY. This is the century of the common man. Anyone in the least unusual is attacked.

LARIA. But this is serious.

CROWLEY. It's nonsense.

URFF comes in. Has just got up. Brown dressing gown, one eye, bedraggled, notebook.

URFF. Letters for me?

CROWLEY. No.

GLORIA. There is one.

CROWLEY. But it's for the great worm. You're not the great worm, are you, Urff?

URFF. Whose number is 654 673 131. One is the great worm.

CROWLEY. Which one? I'll open it. *(There is money in the letter* CROWLEY *opens. No reaction from* URFF.*)*

LARIA. Money!

CROWLEY. Twenty pounds. Cast it on the water, Urff? *(Pause.)* Here.

CROWLEY *passes over Urff's letter to* URFF, *with the money in it.* URFF *trudges off with it. No expression.*

LARIA. This is dangerous! They say they've written to the British Consul in Sicily.

CROWLEY. What can he do? He won't have the power to act.

LARIA. Italy has a Fascist government. They'd love to be seen to be cleaning things up.

CROWLEY. I'm buggered if I'm going back to England. Look at the persecution even a modern novelist like poor Lawrence had to endure—hounded from pillar to post—till he has to leave—branded obscene—all the poor fellow did was to discover the obvious, that nobody in England had thought of, that coal miners had sexual feelings like the rest of us. If they do that to a humble scribbler, what are they going to do to the Logos of the Aeon? We won't go. Don't worry.

GLORIA. Where did Randy disappear to? *(GLORIA goes. She calls off.)* Randy!

LARIA. What if we all discovered our wills, and not just you?

CROWLEY. Religions are autocratic. As my scarlet woman you must have discovered yours. The rest are free to find theirs, or, not. If they find them, they are free in themselves. If they don't know how to look, then they are free to follow the herd.

LARIA. When you were away I missed you. *(CROWLEY nods, satisfied.)* I was sick, but a tall man from the East came for a few days and my strength returned.

CROWLEY. I saw in your diary. There's only one act recorded. How many acts were there?

LARIA. Four, and one which had to be abandoned.

CROWLEY. Must keep up your diary. How's Binky?

LARIA. Pale. She's breathing heavily.

CROWLEY. She's probably just inherited my bronchitis.

LARIA. She clutches at her chest.

CROWLEY. My asthma—

LARIA. Isn't there anything she's inherited from me?

CROWLEY. There are probably plenty of details which we'll see when she grows up, but it needs me to see them.

LARIA. She's not a doll, you know, she's alive and she's not something you made up. She's got a life to lead!

CROWLEY. Laria, I fear very much, that the secret chiefs have decided to let her have her will. The I Ching readings point to only one conclusion. It is her will to die. When I was young, I never thought the path entailed so much suffering. The Secret Chiefs are trying to extinguish one of my selves. *(Decides)* Well, we'll fight them.

LARIA. What with?

CROWLEY. Magick, with a K. We believe every man and every woman is a star, that their being is incandescent, and we must search for power to transform the world. It comes from the self. I transform you. You transform the world, there is nothing apart from the self, the self is. . . everything. *(He gets the pot, squashes, wets it, and begins to daub* LARIA's *back.)*

LARIA. No—she'll be back.

CROWLEY. The rotten potter has left the wheel. God is dead. The pot was a flop.

LARIA. She'll be back.

CROWLEY. You've got a fine big ugly mouth. The best thing about you.

LARIA. She'll think it was me.

CROWLEY. Nothing happens but you two find an excuse to get at each other! *(*CROWLEY *pauses.* URFF *comes back in.)* There is one thing we haven't tried for Binky. Nuttall, by the left had way in the temple. He has always refused—I think he thinks he's got to play the woman. But he's come on a lot in the last couple of days. He got it up and fucked Gloria. . . Urff's current is down. He wouldn't be any good for a magical act.

URFF. I love Laria.

CROWLEY. Love is the law.

URFF. I want to marry her. I think she's the most beautiful woman in the world.

CROWLEY. Urff, you are breaking the law. The law says no trade in human flesh. The scarlet woman must be brazen and **adulterous**.

URFF. That is why.

CROWLEY. She must. She's not to be **married**. That's no good.

URFF. Yes.

LARIA. I don't want to marry him anyway.

URFF. It's true, I'm not worthy of her. I can do the Cabala, but my body isn't up to my brain. My body is a broken reed, but my soul burns with red, blue, green, black, and the numbers 6455231 which designate the great wheel. I'm a shard, a broken wheel. Unless you mend me. According to the law. It says that the scarlet woman shall be adulterous.

CROWLEY. Yes

URFF. Well, how can she be adulterous unless she marries?

CROWLEY. Oh, Urff! Adultery isn't to be taken **literally**. When it says 'adultery' it is drawing the pus from the reeking sewer of bourgeois morality, which will enable the world to embrace The Law.

URFF. Please

CROWLEY. No.

URFF.   It's because I'm not attractive, you see—Laria knows her will and can dominate me. Perhaps if I had some of the beast's musk oil. . .

CROWLEY.   My dear Urff, the oil, correctly used, commands obedience from the bodies around. Smeared on you, it would only be a pathetic request. Concentrate on the worm at the base of your soul. Realize yourself, and you won't have to ask permission to do anything again. Embrace the worm. You are the worm. You have one eye. You are the one-eyed worm.

URFF.   I lost an eye—but that was an accident.

CROWLEY.   Accident? Ha! When have there been accidents!

URFF.   I had a dose of clap, and—

CROWLEY.   Clap in the eye? Good man. Now I know what they mean when they say—'See him off!' You are, with your one eye, the worm. You are the base of creation, the restless, plangent devastating matrix of countless stellar collisions. Your blood is in the stars. The stars are in your blood. Nothingness, with tiny points of light. You pulse, you rave, you roar, you take villages, towns, cities and continents by storm! Burn, rape, pillage, stamp out pity, and the incidental pity for yourself. The uglier, the more hideous gross misshapen you are, the closer to magic comes your every act. The closer you are to magic, which only exists in the night, in the grotesque.

URFF.   But I want Laria because she's beautiful.

CROWLEY.   No, you want her because she's ugly, and because you despise yourself for having sexual feelings, and you despise your body.

URFF.   I quite like fucking, actually.

CROWLEY.   Yes, but—**think**! You have to **think** while you're on the job! Invest it with as much care as any cabalistic problem. That is what it is! Think! You are the worm.

URFF.   I am the worm.

CROWLEY.   I am the Beast. This is my scarlet woman.

URFF.   This is my scarlet woman. *(A correction)* This is the Beast's scarlet woman.

CROWLEY.   Beast tramples on the worm, the worm turns and strikes the beast. Worm, scarlet woman—write—couple—taste. Make an affirmation. Make power by a magical act. Discover your wills. *(Joins their hands, goes out.)*

LARIA.   You are the worm.

URFF.   The worm that turns. The worm in the bud.

LARIA.   This is the work of the beast. *(Shows him mark between breasts.)*

URFF *(peers)*.   He always gets the number of the worm wrong. *(They break from each other.)* Well, Laria, in the Cabala, you cannot describe the essence separately from its numerical quantity. The world is divided into twenty-two essential numbers and any one entity can be described by choosing a sequence of interstices. So it'd be like calling you Mary, or Tom. Because we have names **and** numbers, it's difficult, but when the Law is universal, it'll be much easier—a week'll be. Oneday, Twoday, Threeday, Fourday, Fiveday, Sixday, Sevenday, Eightday, Nineday, and on the twenty-second day, we rest. *(Enters* PETERS. *Moustache, black coat, black hat.)*

PETERS. Hello, I'm the new acolyte. Mr Crowley told me to stand in a thorn bush but I think I'm having heat stroke, so I may have to do it another day. I am extremely interested in what you're doing here. . . What I wanted to know, was, whether you're going to have any orgies today.

URFF. Orgies?

LARIA. What kind of orgies?

PETERS. Where everyone takes their clothes off.

LARIA. People take off their clothes if they're hot. It doesn't mean to say they're going to have an orgy.

PETERS. What else does it mean?

LARIA. Bathing in the sea.

PETERS. Oh. I see. Bathing in the sea with your clothes off.

LARIA. How long are you going to be here?

PETERS. Well, Mr Crowley told me to look at the sun. But I can't follow it anymore. I'm almost blind with watching.

LARIA. Well, are you going to do it?

PETERS. It makes me feel funny. I bet he couldn't follow the sun up and down.

LARIA. That's just the start.

PETERS. I get heatstroke. I think I'll sit in the shade, here.

LARIA. If Frater Perdurabo told you to stand in the sun, he must have had a reason.

PETERS. Sit down. . . in the shade. . . I'd like some water—d'you have any—? *(drinks from pottery bucket)*—just like to sit in the shade a bit—rest—I've come such a long way. But not to stand in the sun. *(CROWLEY appears. Lathering his head and chin with a shaving brush.)*

CROWLEY. If you agreed to stand in the sun, then you can't do anything else.

PETERS. I've been walking all night.

CROWLEY. Off you go. You've embarked on the search for self, and you must submit to the rigours of the course. As you look into the sun. say to yourself, Sanguis et semen. *(Pause. PETERS looks to URFF and LARIA for help, but none comes.)*

PETERS. Sanguis et semen. Sanguis et semen. *(Exists.)*

URFF *(interested).* He's almost fainting!

CROWLEY. We've been carrying too many passengers. Urff, detain Nuttall at all costs when he comes in from the sea. Don't let him off into the hills.

URFF. How?

CROWLEY. Seduce him with your charm.

URFF. I don't have any.

CROWLEY. The flies are attracted to you, Urff, there must be something there. *(Exits.)*

URFF. Why does everybody persecute me? I don't like being persecuted. I want to marry you, Laria. Then you can be adulterous. I wouldn't mind which whore I was married to—you, or Gloria. . . but I would like to be married to someone, so that I could be free.

LARIA. Free for what?

URFF. So that I could say, you're mine, you mustn't do that, when they are bad, and they could beat me for obstructing their will.

LARIA. That's the wrong way round. That's how the world does it.

URFF. I have this need, for people to see me as a worm.

LARIA. You are a worm. The Beast told you.

URFF. He wants me to be a big worm, and I'm really small. He wants me to rear myself up on end, but I want to go along the ground, that your heel shall crush my head. I can't rebel, like worm ought to.

LARIA. The Will is rebellion. The weak are crushed.

URFF. Teach me how to rebel.

LARIA. You are weak because you despise yourself, and are divided.

URFF. Yes, but which half must I obliterate.

LARIA. One must eat the other up.

URFF. The worm must eat up the self.

LARIA. Now as happens all the time.

URFF. Teach me. Teach the worm how to rebel.

LARIA. You can't teach it, you can only learn it.

URFF. The way I wish to learn it, is to be beaten again, by you extremely hard. Sanguis et semen ad terram spiritum conferrat. Smother me till one or the other rebels. Stamp on my face. Bury me deep in the earth. One or another will conquer, I will become whole. Take the skin off my back and cram it in my mouth. I can't find me. I'm lost—pity me. Kick my teeth in.

LARIA. No.

URFF. You would do it willingly if you knew how I felt!

LARIA. You wouldn't ask, if you knew how I felt!

URFF. It is my will that it is done!

LARIA. It doesn't help! It doesn't help! You've got a twisted personality, Urff, and there's nothing I can do! I don't **know** how to help you find your true self, but it's not like that! Not by making me go through torment!

URFF. Well, what do you do with the Beast?

18

LARIA. He's strong! He allows himself to be tied, because he is
   strong! But you want to be tied because you're weak!
URFF. Damn you! Damn you!

He starts slowly to kick, punch and bite himself, glowering at
LARIA. GLORIA *comes in with a bowl of henna.* LARIA *and*
GLORIA *ignore* URFF.
Tableau with URFF *kicking, biting and so on for ten seconds.*
Blood comes out of his mouth. He stands forward to them.

URFF. I've done it. I've bitten my tongue. Look. I'll bleed
   to death, now, and then you'll be sorry. *(Neither of them looks.*
   He goes. GLORIA *mixing up henna in bowl.)*
GLORIA. My arms are so sore.
LARIA. What's the matter?
GLORIA. We had a first person singular pruning session.
LARIA. Don't let him make you lose blood on that. I mean,
   we're not children.
GLORIA. I hate the smell of this stuff.
LARIA. Henna is good for one's hair and it turns it red which is
   the colour of haloes, colour of the sun.
GLORIA. Well, mine goes maroon. *(Pause)*
LARIA. Why do we quarrel over this man if we know that love is
   not possession? *(Pause)*
GLORIA. I don't know. Lust?
LARIA. Lust is work. Surely we're not quarrelling over work like a
   couple of secretaries. . .
GLORIA. I—
LARIA. One. . .
GLORIA. One doesn't know.
LARIA. You'll get used to it. We have not secrets. We're all bound
   for glory.
GLORIA. Three's a difficult number.
LARIA. The Beast would like to have four wives, like in the Koran.
   I keep pointing out to him that he does if he counts the men. It is
   strange that after all the fights one goes through in the name of
   freedom that one always comes back to the family whether you
   want to or not. Here we are, from the far corners of the world,
   thinking we're independent of our past, and in reality we're all
   just like Urff. Banging our heads against the wall. If I had a
   better past to return to I'd go there. You don't understand that,
   do you? You want to be his number one. Well, I'm his number
   one. Whether Binky lives or dies and if you don't like it you and
   Randy can fuck off back where you came from. (RANDY *rushes*
   on.)
RANDY. I'm going to be the Beast! I've seen a sign! I've seen a sign!
GLORIA. What was the sign, dear?
RANDY. Satan! He's dead in the gully with his tongue out and I

can tell it's a sign because his eyes are open and he's shit
himself and has anyone got a pickaxe?

GLORIA. Why do you want a pickaxe?

RANDY. I want a pickaxe! So I can bury him. *(GLORIA gets him a pickaxe.)*

GLORIA. Alright, dear, go on.

RANDY. I want to bury him so that no one else will see him and
his yeeargh face and body all swollen up and all the power and
the flies will be mine. He's been shot through the tummy so that
his guts are coming out but I'll put them back in so that he can
serve me. He'll always be behind me. I shall be the Beast! *(Goes.)*

GLORIA. There's a good boy.

CROWLEY *comes out pursued by* URFF.
CROWLEY *oiling himself, in bathrobe.*

CROWLEY. Where's sailor Boy Nuttall?

GLORIA. No one's seen him.

URFF. Take me! You said you liked ugly people!

CROWLEY. Go and read the Liber Legis, Urff. You're under
everyone's feet! You've got to take me when you're ready.

URFF. Ha! That's it! Always talking as if you were Jesus bloody
Christ and I was some turd you'd stepped on in the street!

CROWLEY. Turd is about it, Urff.

URFF. Worms! Turds! Can't I scrape comparison with humanity?

CROWLEY. There's no such thing. They don't exist, they're
ciphers like Tarot cards. You're a worm. Learn to live with
unreality.

URFF. That man getting sunstroke out there is real.

CROWLEY. Nonsense. *(Pause)* I invoke Nuttall. My spirit
summons Nuttall. *(Incanting)* Nuttall, become material.
Arise from the vasty deep. *(NUTTALL comes in. Lightly)*
Ah, Frater Omnia Smegmam. Refresh yourself with a little
cocaine.

NUTTALL. I have sent the telegram. And I asked for four
hundred pounds.

CROWLEY. What a bold man you are, against your father.

NUTTALL *(taking cocaine).* Oh, this is such a great pleasure
it's unnatural.

CROWLEY. It heals the sick, Nuttall, it raises the dead.

NUTTALL. My father has heard of you. Once—your name
was in discussion. He said he had heard that Somerset Maugham
had based a book on you.

CROWLEY *(delighted).* Yes! He did! Young Maugham came to
Paris—we all thought he was terribly green and couldn't lay
one whore in front of another—but it turned out the puppy
could write.

NUTTALL. It was common gossip that it was a portrait of you.

CROWLEY. I told Maugham I ate babies. From the extremities
in order to save the tasty bits to the end. The only man who
didn't believe me was Frank Harris.

NUTTALL. Is he a friend of yours too?

CROWLEY. Oh yes. He was.

NUTTALL. My father said he was a bad man too. *(RANDY
enters and watches from the back.)*

CROWLEY. No doubt at all. He was a journalist. You see what
journalism is doing to us.

NUTTALL. My father said Frank Harris took advantage of over
10,000 women. Is it true?

CROWLEY. Of course. Why does your father not like you?

NUTTALL. I've never been able to live up to his idea of me.

CROWLEY. How does it feel in there? *(Peers at NUTTALL.)*

NUTTALL. Good. Yes, very good. *(NUTTALL is high. He
sniffs again.)*

CROWLEY. A little brandy? *(He drinks.)* A little more brandy?
(They all watch NUTTALL.) What is the Law?

NUTTALL. Love and do what thou wilt.

CROWLEY. That's St. Augustine's law. What's ours?

NUTTALL. Do what thou wilt shall be the whole of the Law.
*(NUTTALL goes downstage. PETERS comes in. Still has
overcoat on.)*

PETERS. The sun. . . The sun *(PETERS stands centre stage.)*

NUTTALL. This man is **death**. Is going to take your daughter
away.

PETERS. Take me in.

GLORIA. D'you want a drink?

PETERS. Take me in, Please.

NUTTALL. **Don't** let him in! Resist evil. This man is to take
your daughter away. Can't you see, you fools, he's dressed in
black? Don't do it. Get him off before he forces your hand. He's
come to take your daughter away. Off the premises. . .
(NUTTALL is warming to his theme of bearing witness.)

PETERS. Sun. Sun. . . sun.

NUTTALL. Get out! Leave Binky alone.

PETERS. Who?

CROWLEY. He's a neophyte, Nuttall, not a baby snatcher.

NUTTALL. I must impress on you all the importance in rejecting
death from your doorstep. Death is not part of our natures. He is
an invasion. The Abbey must become a fortress. It's not just Binky.
It's all of us.

CROWLEY. You're rambling, Nuttall. Come to the Temple with me.

NUTTALL. Though he'll start with the weakest—the little baby. We
must eject the intruder.

LARIA. What do you want with us. *(Nervous)* Where are you from?

PETERS. The sun. . . please. . . it's too difficult. . . the sun. . .

poor Peters.

NUTTALL. The rock! Ha! The rock! We're floundering! We've been holed by Christianity! Don't you see? He's called **Peters**! The rock! Keep him out! Keep death out! Brain him, kill him! Strangle him! Chase him, wipe him out! Kill! Kill! Kill! The rock! The rock!

NUTTALL *has concluded bearing witness and retires upstage, but* LARIA *has been taken over by his message.*
She flings herslef at PETERS *in a frenzy. Quickly* CROWLEY *pulls her off.*

LARIA. Go away! Go away!

PETERS. The sun. . . *(PETERS is lying collapsed downstage.)*

URFF. You'd never do that for me—

CROWLEY. Do you want to come in out of the sun?

GLORIA. Randy, get him some water. *(RANDY goes and gets the water,* LARIA *weeping, exits with* CROWLEY. URFF *exits.)*

PETERS. I have come from far away.

GLORIA. Would you like a drink?

PETERS. I close my eyes and I can see dancing. . .

RANDY *comes back, gives* PETER *water.* PETERS *sits up, begins recovery.*

GLORIA. You can stay as long as you like.

PETERS. Thank Christ for that.

GLORIA. Where did you hear of us?

PETERS. When I was in Venice.

GLORIA. When were you there?

PETERS. Earlier.

GLORIA. What did you see there?

PETERS. Mostly water.

GLORIA. You don't like architecture.

PETERS. It keeps the rain off.

RANDY. Where you from?

PETERS. Hi, shorty. *(At large)* The whores in Venice are amazing. They hang around the street corners treading water. The ones who haven't learnt to swim have waterwings. D'you have waterwings, sonny?

RANDY. Answer the fucking question!!

PETERS. Er—I'm a magician. I live on my wits, not off other people's shit. *(Mysterious)* And I come from the astral plane, sonny.

RANDY. Show me a trick.

PETERS. I will make a talking white mouse.

RANDY. What d'you need?

PETERS. Whatever you use round here.

RANDY. We use sex magic round here to get what we want.

PETERS. Is this what you want? *(Gestures to the Abbey)*

22

RANDY. Yeah.

PETERS. Humble, for magicians.

RANDY. Get on with it.

PETERS. I need a jug of iced water, a loaf of bread, and a piece of cheese.

RANDY. That's a meal! I want to talk white mouse.

PETERS. You'll get it.

He tries Nora's nut cutlets, and pockets one for later.
RANDY *goes and get a small piece of bread and soft cheese.*

RANDY. Right! Make a mouse. *(PETERS starts eating.)* Hey!

PETERS. Well, you do sex magic, I do eat magic. Now you see it, now you don't.

RANDY. Is it a magic mouse?

PETERS. It is. It belongs to me and it can make itself appear and disappear. When it smells the cheese, it'll come.

RANDY. Is it your guardian angel?

PETERS *(bluffing).* Er... This here little mouse has got me out of more scrapes than you've had hot dinners. More nous in its snout than you have in the whole of your body, small fry.

RANDY. A dog serves me called Satan. He'll eat up the mouse.

PETERS. Oh yeah? *(Finishing)* The mouse is ready to come out.

RANDY. Are you putting all your power in the mouse?

PETERS. I am, little poxer. All my power. *(we see RANDY has a hammer behind his back. PETER fiddles.)* There she is. Isn't she sweet? Zooe, she's called. Sweet little mouse, even though every minute she pisses in my pocket.
(RANDY smashes the hammer down on the mouse.)

RANDY. Gotcha!

PETERS. Hey!

RANDY. The power's mine.

GLORIA. Be nice to him, Randy! *(RANDY scoops something into his mouth and rushes off.)* He—didn't **eat** it. . .? Is the mouse alright?

PETERS *(amazed).* I would have thought it was a bit underdone, myself.

GLORIA. Oh no! He hasn't eaten it alive! **Alive!**

PETERS. Well. . . He did stun it first. *(Pause)*

GLORIA. How could he! Ugh! I hate mice.

PETERS. I was fond of Zooe.

GLORIA *(disgust).* You kept her in your pocket?

PETERS. Poor Zooe. Mouse torturer! *(He takes his coat off. Very dirty sailor uniform underneath. GLORIA looks at the uniform.)*

GLORIA. What's **this**?

PETERS. I was trying to decide if you'd turn me in.

GLORIA. You're a deserter.

PETERS. I am the only person in the world who must have been stupid enough to jump ship in Venice. I had to swim down about eighty miles of canals.

GLORIA. D'you know where you are?

PETERS. Yeah, Sicily.

GLORIA. This is the Abbey of Thelema!

PETERS. Looks like a piss-poor barn, to me . . .

GLORIA. No! We're famous.

PETERS. No kidding.

GLORIA. Here we are—look—*(newspaper)*

PETERS *(reads)*. Black shit and corruption. Orgies! At last! I was right! 'Aleister Crowley the notorious satanist has threatened the Pax Britannica of the Mediterranean by his presence. . . at any moment the British Consulate may well receive reports of enraged Sicilians taking the matter into their hands.' Yeah, they get that trouble in New York.

CROWLEY *enters, rouged mouth, earrings, greased, purple robe, bare arms, head shaven. Slides into a seat near* PETERS.

CROWLEY *(salacious)*. Love is the law, love under will. How do you do? Peters, welcome to the Abbey.

PETERS. I've been reading about you.

CROWLEY. It is no substitute for direct experience. Gloria, could you prepare Peter's room?

GLORIA. Which one?

CROWLEY. Nuttall's. I'm afraid he hasn't measured up to the severe standards of selfhood. I'm going to put Peters to the test, since he's here. *(*GLORIA *leaves.)* What brings you here, Peters?

PETERS. A mistake.

CROWLEY. There are no mistakes.

PETERS. Randy's just had my mouse. I hope that was a mistake.

CROWLEY. What we in our ignorance call 'blind chance' are in fact the activities of the Secret Chiefs. I have learnt to submit my will to theirs because they tell me I have a mission. I have been broken so repeatedly in the course of my life that I no longer have a continuous character at all. Very soon I shall become pure Being. Freed from the bonds which tie it to earth the conscious moves through matter like mist through a veil. So, you're a sailor.

PETERS. I was. I jumped ship.

CROWLEY. What date? Can we tell anything from the date. . . ?

PETERS. I dunno. It was spring I guess. I've been walking round. It's been a lot easier recently with the peaches ripe.

CROWLEY. What do you know about magic?

PETERS. The one trick I had has been called out.

CROWLEY. Magic consists of altering the known world by certain rituals and acts, which are connected to the state of affairs in the astral plane, which interpenetrates everything. Do you follow me?

PETERS. Right.

CROWLEY. Conventional magic is dependent on lengthy preparation, expensive materials, and a lifetime's investigation would not unravel half of what is practised. In 1890 I discovered the left hand way..

PETERS. No kidding.

CROWLEY. The left had way democratises magic because it places in our hands—literally—in our **bodies** all the power we need. By specific acts of sex magic one can effect changes in the physical world. I want health for my daughter. And life, and love and laughter. Not death, which is indicated for her. In this act, which you have been sent here to accomplish with me, you will go with me to the temple, in order to assure my daughter's safety. *(PETERS looks at newspapers.)*

PETERS. Do you really do this with drugs?

CROWLEY. Drugs are used simply to heighten the sense of awareness. The Christian, by alienating himself from the Dionysiac founts in the person, cuts off his nose to spite his face. And who wants to go through life without a nose?

PETERS. Who indeed?

CROWLEY. Who?

PETERS. Who? *(CROWLEY and PETERS snort cocaine. PETERS getting gradually higher.)*

CROWLEY. The no-nose brigade are prevalent, prurient moralists, moral syphilitics. There is a child sick. We must create life force. Prana. A mixture of blood and semen which I was as the father will consume. The semen will be yours. I shall be your woman. You take me anally, and the blood comes from the third finger of the left hand of both of us, a mere pinprick, I assure you.

PETERS. What am I letting myself in for?

CROWLEY. Well, it's no loss to your dignity. If the Secret Chiefs plan to send you away, I imagine you will be on your feet and through the gate in a flash.

PETERS. In the navy we used to do quite a lot of the, er, left hand way, but it was usually with petty officers, to get extra shore leaves.

CROWLEY. I am asking you as one man to another. Save my child.

PETERS. So, they got wind of the kind of things you do, and they're trying to close you down. Is that right?

CROWLEY. Never mind the Abbey. Save the child.

PETERS. I want to get throughout smashed first.

CROWLEY. You've got to be able to concentrate.

PETERS. How old are you?

CROWLEY. What does it matter? I'm fifty.

PETERS. You're exactly twice my age.

CROWLEY.   How do you find your way here?

PETERS *(sagacious)*.   Oh by the moon and stars now less. The Dog Star.

CROWLEY.   The eye of Sirius Dog Star. Dog. Satan drawing you on. Red from the sky.

PETERS.   No it wasn't Satan, it was the fucking Dog Star. And when I was in Palermo I went into a pet shop to ask directions. They got me some breakfast, and what the hell, I stole this mouse called Zooe. Then your little boy killed it.

CROWLEY.   Not my little boy.

PETERS.   I reckoned that mouse was looking after me.

CROWLEY.   We all have guardians. It's true. My guardian angel is called Aiwass, he dictated Liber Legis to me in Cairo in 1904.

PETERS.   Liber Legis? What's that?

CROWLEY.   It's a book. I'll tell you about it another time. We must get to work before the sun passes its zenith. *(They stand.)*

PETERS.   What do I get for this, anyhow? That kid squashed my mouse, the only true friend I had. And you want me to think of you as a **magician**?

CROWLEY.   Look into my eyes. D'you doubt it? *(PETERS looks and quails a little.)*

PETERS.   But why'd he kill my mouse? What do I get out of this, anyhow? And who wants it at twelve o'clock? What are we going to **do** all afternoon?

CROWLEY.   Work. *(He leads him off)* Work, work, and more work.

NUTTALL, *alone, ruminative.*
URFF *comes in.*

URFF *(to* NUTTALL*)*.   There are no limits to pain, to agony. I cannot find the means to let go of my self and become universal. Suffering is as great as the universe, which is infinite. Nuttall, I am on the dark side of the moon. There are no limits to what can happen here. I cannot abandon my self-respect or my miserable humanity. The Cabala predicts an endless sequence of numbers in response to my questions about suffering. They stretch without a break to the horizon. When shall I make a compact with the night, and the man who is my oppressor?

NUTTALL *(knowing)*.   The Beast.

URFF.   Did I choose him, or did he choose me?

NUTTALL.   You are the worm, he is the Beast. That is all we know, and all we need to know. I have not been here long enough to discover my will. But it's coming.

URFF.   But even he suffers. He is in agony from addiction, and his child's dying. If I'm struggling to get into his position, what will I know any different when I'm there?

NUTTALL.   I don't understand it, either. The devil suffers. What

26

does God do about it? He doesn't put him out of his misery.
    (LARIA enters with bundle, nursing it.)
NUTTALL. Is there anything the matter, Laria?
LARIA. Binky's dead.
URFF *(pious).* Blessed relief from suffering. . .
LARIA *(flatly).* Binky's dead.
NUTTALL. What, just now? *(Pause)* Oh, that's . . . tragic.
    That's . . . unfortunate, *(GLORIA enters.)*
GLORIA. What's up?
NUTTALL. Binky's dead. *(GLORIA goes and suddenly puts her arms
    around LARIA.)*
GLORIA. I'm sorry. I'm ever so sorry. *(LARIA starts to cry and
    GLORIA comforts her.)*
NUTTALL. Shouldn't someone fetch the Beast? He won't like being
    interrupted, but there's not much point now, in **that** magical
    operation, unless he's trying to bring the dead back to life.

NORA HENESSEY *enters, blithely oblivious. She flops down at the
table, carrying a wilting bunch of wild flowers. RANDY follows her
in and stops a short distance away. He is carrying the pickaxe. He
glowers at NORA.*

NORA. You've been digging, Randy. Well done! What have you
    been digging?
URFF *(to NUTTALL).* He shouldn't do that, you know. The dead
    should rest in peace.
NORA. I had this idea, that one could subsist solely on the visions
    which the Mediterranean vista provides. I would have loved to have
    been one of the first anchorites and stared over a deserted sea.
    (Pause) It's so hot, though! Randy, would you get some water for
    my flowers? Let's hope it's not too late. *(RANDY exits and
    NORA inspects the table. She examines the nut cutlets and finds
    some letters addressed to her. Pleased)* For me. *(She begins open-
    ing them)* And someone's had a nibble of my little offering, I
    see. Was that you, Urff?
URFF *(torn between clearing his name and breaking Coventry).* Er,
    no.
NUTTALL *(to URFF).* Sshh!
NORA. I'll get you all to talk, yet. *(RANDY comes in with water.)*
    Little Randy responds to kindness, don't you? Thank you,
    darling.

RANDY *takes up the pickaxe and moves to see what LARIA is
holding. He peers over GLORIA'S shoulder.*

GLORIA *(fierce, low).* Go away.
NORA. And he had the good sense to talk to me when no one was
    about. And yet, it's a tragedy in the making that he doesn't
    know his ABC's. *(Staring at GLORIA'S back)* And we all know at

whose feet to lay that particular tragedy. *(NORA reading the letter.)*

NUTALL. Wasn't it the Beast who said Randy needn't learn to read?

URFF. That's right.

NUTTALL. It's nothing to do with Gloria, then. Any more than the rest of us. We're meant to be a commune, so we're all collectively responsible. I personally think he should learn to read.

URFF. Then why did the Beast get his way? *(Pause.)*

NORA *looks up from her letter.*

NORA *(announcement).* I'm sorry to say, everybody, that my mother has been taken rather ill. In fact, she's very poorly. This means I shall be obliged to go home, with all speed. There's another letter here, but it's not addressed to anybody. *(NUTTALL takes the proffered envelope. Turns it over URFF examining it closely.)* Yes. I didn't think mother would last out the year, somehow. I had a premonition.

NORA *exits.*
URFF *and* NUTTALL *are wrapped up in the problem of the letter with no name on it.*

URFF. Things happen in threes. . . *(NUTTALL decides to cut the Gordian knot.)* Shouldn't the Beast?

NUTTALL *(opening the letter).* It doesn't matter who opens it. The bad news is going to be the same, if it is bad news. . . *(They study an official looking document which has come in the letter.)* It's in Italian. *(Gives it to URFF)* You're the linguist. *(URFF doesn't want the job of reading the letter.)*

URFF. Only Hebrew and Greek.

NUTTALL. Come on. Italian's only Latin. *(URFF reads.)*

URFF. It's from the police. It's a deportation order.

NUTTALL. Oh, god. Why?

URFF. It doesn't say.

NUTTALL. I suppose we'll have to go. Gloria, they're chucking us out.

GLORIA. What? *(She gets up from LARIA'S side and looks at the letter in URFF'S hand.)* The fascist bastards.

NUTTALL *(proud).* My father has **always** mistrusted Mussolini. He told me when I said I was going to Italy. He said, 'That man's crazy.' Fascists. . . You can't expect them to behave like civilised human beings now *(CROWLEY enters as before in drag. But he knows there's something wrong.)* There's bad news, I'm afraid. Binky's dead.

CROWLEY. I know. *(Pause)*

28

NUTTALL *(surprised)*. Did you? *(PETERS enters looking sheepish)*

URFF *(sure of himself)*. Peters couldn't get it up, is that right?

CROWLEY. I'm sorry, Laria. Fate was stronger than desire.

NUTTALL. What's he talking about?

URFF. The magical act with Peters to save Binky's life. Peters couldn't get it up.

NUTTALL. Oh, I see. . .

PETERS *(ingratiating)*. Sorry.

CROWLEY *(to LARIA)*. We were checkmate by the secret chiefs. They wanted her. Don't cry.

LARIA *begins to cry and sob. CROWLEY behind her, his hand on her shoulder.*

NORA HENESSEY *re-enters, with a suitcase.*

NORA. I've had my things packed now for a number of days, but I always thought that what sent me away would come from within the group. Mr Crowley, I am leaving. My mother is not well. One should look after one's family. I am leaving.

CROWLEY. Good. *(No one will look at her.)*

NORA *(desperate)*. Goodbye. *(Pause)* Anyway, I'm glad. I'm not sure I want to stay around in this pigsty to see your daughter die for lack of proper medical attention, while you caper around like the Queen of Sheba.

NUTTALL. Binky is dead. *(Points to LARIA)*

NORA. Well, then, that only proves my point.

CROWLEY. Get out.

NORA. I didn't mean that. I'm sorry, that was harsh. But it's no harsher than the punishment you decided to give me. *(Pause)* Mr. Crowley, you owe me a hundred pounds.

CROWLEY. Peters, would you take this woman's bags to the village?

PETERS *(overeager)*. Yes, Sir! *(He bustles up and takes them officiously and stands next to NORA, smiling brightly.)*

PETERS. Ready to go, Ma'am?

NORA *(cold)*. Who are you?

PETERS. I'm just a nobody.

NORA. Come alone then. *(They exit slowly.)*

LARIA *(to CROWLEY)*. Why are they throwing us out?

CROWLEY *(softly)*. It is written, it is the destiny of Alastor, the Wanderer of the Waste. . .

URFF. You were right, you know, about Peters being an incarnation.

NUTTALL *(to URFF)*. How d'you know he was an incarnation?

URFF. He said as much to Nora. He said, 'I am Nobody.'

NUTTALL. I see. If he wasn't anybody, then who was he?

URFF. Precisely!

NUTTALL. I wonder if he's still visible, then. He might have evaporated, when he left.

He exits, curious to see. URFF strikes a casual, knowing pose, as if he was above chasing phantoms and turns and watches CROWLEY and LARIA.
GLORIA, sensitive to the mood of the moment, leaves LARIA and exits.

URFF. Poor Binky. Makes you wish there was a heaven, doesn't it.
LARIA. I want to die. *(Insistent)* I want to die.
URFF. Yes, yes.

Although excluded, URFF nods sympathetically and walks off slowly. CROWLEY and LARIA oblivious.
The last member of the group is RANDY. He stares at the backs of CROWLEY and LARIA darkly.

CROWLEY. We shall make new life from the ruins of the old.
   (Becomes aware of RANDY.) What is it, Randy? *(RANDY holds out the pickaxe. He wants to help bury the baby.)*
LARIA *(losing control).*   Go away, you little monster! Go away!

RANDY exits, dropping the pickaxe, hurried, frightened by LARIA'S screaming at him.
LARIA subsides, hugging the bundle and weeping.

CROWLEY. It's simple. We have to make better fortune
   for ourselves. Put the child down.

CROWLEY is making strong and clear sexual advances to LARIA, very much the boss in the situation. But he can't make her let go of the bundle with BINKY inside.

CROWLEY. Come. We have work to do.

He pins her on the table. The lights are dying fast. Music, sudden, loud, conclusive.
LARIA screams one scream to the blackout: rage, surrender, grief, sorrow, a great scream. CROWLEY keeps pushing. She still holds BINKY.

CROWLEY. *(of the scream).*   That's better.

Blackout.

ACT TWO

*Set suggests ballroom or decaying dining-room of a once grand hotel,
with huge, shabby dim mirrors. Assorted tables, white cloths covering
some of them, but overall a great deal of open space.
CROWLEY is seated at one of the tables. He has a kilt or tartan
trousers and a glengarry cap on, and a large dark coat.
LARIA enters dusting off a large elderly menu.
She is dressed in a flame red (or what you will) costume and heavily
made up as the scarlet woman. The time is a few weeks after Act
One concluded and the place is the Hotel Christol in Boulogne.
LARIA sits down with CROWLEY who takes the menu.*

LARIA.   The last boat leaves Boulogne for England in four hours.
CROWLEY.   There's time for supper if they'd only serve us.
LARIA.   We've only got enough money for the boat.
CROWLEY.   That gendarme who's been prowling around told me
   to stay in here or I'd get arrested.
LARIA.   I've just been talking to him. He thinks you're Gerard
   Lee Bevan the bank robber.

CROWLEY *tries to attract the attention of a Maitre D', who crosses the
   stage without looking at either of them. He fails.*

CROWLEY.   If they'd only give us some supper, I wouldn't grudge
   them their little game.
LARIA.   I think I could get us out of here, if I could just get him on
   his own. But she doesn't like him talking to me.

DIDEROT, *the police commissioner, crosses the stage and* LARIA
smiles and waves at him. He smiles smarmily back and approaches.
DIDEROT *stands behind* CROWLEY *who pretends that the policeman
is in fact a waiter.*
DIDEROT *gets out their passports.*

CROWLEY.   Well, which wine would you recommend?
DIDEROT.   Name, please.
CROWLEY.   Aleister Crowley.
DIDEROT.   Madame?

LARIA. Maine, Laria Maine, M-A-I-N-E. Got it?

DIDEROT *(interested)*. So you are not married?

CROWLEY. No. We're not married. And I want my dinner.

DIDEROT. I would like you to come separately and identify your belongings.

LARIA. Are we clean?

CROWLEY. Absolutely. I finished everything.

DIDEROT. It's a very small matter. I need to talk to Madame. *(DIDEROT smirks.)*

LARIA. I'm not. . . *(To CROWLEY)* I can't. Not with him. He's just too repulsive. *(DIDEROT tugs at LARIA'S sleeve and she reluctantly goes, hurried off by him.)*

DIDEROT. Come. Come.

The exquisitely dressed MAITRE D' comes in and places two glasses at CROWLEY'S table, filling one with brandy. Then, he stands by. MADAME POITIER enters. Handsome, coiffed, Haute Bourgeoise, fifties. She begins immediately.

MME POITIER. We owe you an apology, Mr Crowley. *(She speaks English without an accent)* I'm afraid my English is rusty—I spent some time in England, but that was many years ago. However, everyone has heard of the famous Mr Aleister Crowley. So while the police are filling out their reports—it will be a pleasure to provide you with supper free of charge.

CROWLEY. I'll have roast beef and '93 Hautbrion. *(She takes the menu and gives it to the MAITRE D', who exits.)*

MME POITIER. Again, I apologize. The menu you were given is out of date. There is only one menu tonight. I did not realize that you were the Aleister Crowley, but one of our older lady residents recognized you when you came in.

CROWLEY. Who's this woman? I didn't see anyone.

MME POITIER. Oh, she's a rich old widow who occupies the top floor.

CROWLEY. Is she interested in the occult?

MME POITIER. She is. She said you used to be a mountaineer.

CROWLEY. Yes. Extremely. . . rich?

MME POITIER. Oh, yes.

CROWLEY. Would you ask her to take supper with me?

MME POITIER. Certainly. She said something strange. She said that there had been an accident once when you were climbing, and you had saved yourself by walking away. Others hadn't been so lucky. I'm sorry we don't have the right menu. We'll recover, but we went downhill after the war.

CROWLEY. You weren't the manager here before. How long have you been the manager?

MME POITIER. Since the patron died. He was a lovely man. We had a wonderful marriage. Marriage is a serious business for us bourgeoises. I'm as married again now, but it's not the same. . . You're such an unusual man. Tell me, were your parents married?

CROWLEY. Yes indeed. To each other.

MME POITIER. And do you take after your father?

CROWLEY. No. He was a preacher, a fundamentalist. He believed that the world was created in 4004 BC by God, who popped fossils in the rocks in order to tempt the faithful to unbelief.

MME POITIER. And you're not like that at all, is that what you are saying?

CROWLEY. I'm the Logos of the Aeon. The new era started in 1904. Now, by force of my will, come unafraid, out of the yawning cavities, the creatures of the night. The only sin is restriction. *(MME POITIER pours CROWLEY some brandy.)*

MME POITIER. So, you are a prophet and a mountaineer and an anti-marriageist. How intriguing.

CROWLEY. And a poet.

MME POITIER. But that is wonderful!

CROWLEY. Yes, but the old labels won't do any more.

MME POITIER. So how would you describe yourself in the new way?

CROWLEY. As a Magus, that is to say the incarnation and culmination of ten thousand years of magical tradition reaching back to the Babylonians through countless figures like Newton and Paracelsus. But my face to the modern age is that of a psychologist.

MME POITIER. A psychologist! Yes, that is modern!

CROWLEY. People oppose me now, but in my own day I shall be believed, and remorse will disappear.

MME POITIER. When did you discover that you were different?

CROWLEY. When I discovered sex. I was twelve. I fucked one of the servants. She got the sack and I got enlightenment.

MME POITIER. And what happened to her?

CROWLEY. She went to London and turned herself into a whore, I expect. Hardly a great change. Most of them did, the worthless ones who were dismissed without references. . . She was called Ann Chapman.

MME POITIER. Ann Chapman. . . I was trained at the Savoy, that's where I learned my English, it was exactly the same time, thirty-five years ago. I lived in London in the most abject poverty— terrifying! One of Jack the Ripper's murders was committed just around the corner. I lay in the bedbugs and dreamed of being a great hotelier.

CROWELY. Well, what are you now?

MME POITIER *(suave)*. A great hotelier. You should meet this woman You might get something from her.

CROWLEY. . . . . Is she. . . very rich?

MME POITIER. She's very impatient to meet you, the Great Magician. *(Pause.)*

CROWLEY. Let her wait. You were in London then. Did you **understand** the Jack the Ripper murders?

MME POITIER. Some mindless animal with bloodlust. . .

CROWLEY. No. It was a magical operation. To obtain supreme power.

MME POITIER. With ordinary whores, picked at random?

CROWLEY. There's nothing wrong with the ordinariness of whores—that's precisely why they were chosen—and each murder makes power: their bodies formed a calvary cross of seven points, stretching across London facing the west. The point is after the fourth killing, the police reached the woman as she was still literally screaming her guts out in a cul de sac. There was no possible escape—but the magician has acquired the power of invisibility. He has literally disappeared. The fourth killing confers the power of invisibility. Then the kills grow more frequent, because he has nothing to fear. (CROWLEY *has drawn a Calvary cross in the dust on a table top.)*

POITIER. He. . . ?

CROWLEY. After the seventh, the magician stops, because his task has been accomplished. The calvary cross is complete.

MME POITIER. There was a theory that he was an ex-officer.

CROWLEY. Yes. He went around in evening wear, so that after he had dined off the more succulent portions of the ladies, he turns up his collar—and not a trace remains to be seen.

POITIER. Are you sure it wasn't you who did it?

CROWLEY. No, it wasn't me. My mission is to abolish the difference between the dark and the light. That's my vocation.

MME POITIER. You think that Jack the Ripper would be a stronger magician than you?

CROWLEY. Quite possibly. Either you have knowledge, or you have power. In recent years, I have concentrated on knowledge. I used to blast other magicians. I blasted McGregor Mathers once.

MME POITIER. You killed him?

CROWLEY. I blasted him. He had led the Order of the Golden Dawn disastrously astray. I had to do it, to save the Order.

MME POITIER. But—how many people have you actually killed intentionally?

CROWLEY. I'm afraid that I have no idea of what you mean by intention. Everything I do, I do with my whole being. My conscious and unconscious are integrated.

MME POITIER. These four men who fell off your rope in the Himalayas, were you responsible? *(Pause.)* And we have all followed your amusing adventures at Cefalu where I understand you were expelled after you were discovered eating a baby. *(CROWLEY laughs.)* Your baby. *(CROWLEY is pleased.)*

CROWLEY. It's very flattering to have other people's wish-fulfilments projected onto me, but I can't live up to that one. The child was ill. She died. That was all. We buried her.

MME POITIER. Why couldn't you save her?

CROWLEY. I tried everything. But then again, there's probably a little bit of me that wanted her to die.

MME POITIER. You had a death-wish for your daughter?

CROWLEY. Obviously. How else could she die?

MME POITIER. So if I could summarize, you claim to be a supreme magus and to have abolished the differences between the dark and the light, yin and yang, consciousness and unconsciousness. This puts you in a position of unique responsibility with regard to those around you, because if they die, you can be said to have willed it.

CROWLEY. Yes. Again, if there are shortcomings in my example, this does not mean that the Law is affected. The Law of Do What Thou Wilt.

MME POITIER. Let us suppose that say, Jack the Ripper had a complete idea of what he was doing, and took full responsibility. If he was doing it for a purpose, would he be a greater magician than you?

CROWLEY. Seven of hearts always outbids five of hearts. But then, there is always the element of strategy. Magic is like anything else. It's never quite a straight fight. *(Stands up.)* I've enjoyed talking to you. But I must go to work, if we're going to catch the last boat.

MME POITIER. No, wait, please! When did the new era start?

CROWLEY. 1904. My guardian angel Aiwass dictated the Book of the Law to me then. This is very good brandy.

MME POITIER. Yes. It comes from the Marne. '88 was a bad year for the champagne but a good year for brandy.

CROWLEY. The year of the Ripper.

MME POITIER. Has London changed?

CROWLEY. It gets bigger, I hear. . .

MME POITIER *(waving brandy glass)*. Isn't it amazing that some of the Ripper's victims must have died as these sour little grapes were being picked? I am very curious about a possible connection between you and Jack the Ripper. The servant who was dismissed after you had to do with her. . .

CROWLEY. Ann Chapman.

MME. POITIER. A woman of the same name was killed just around the corner from me, when I was in London, eighth of September, 1888.

CROWLEY. It's plausible to imagine her working as a whore two years after her dismissal. I remember my mother refused to give her a reference, point-blank.

MME POITIER. But the Ripper murders aren't sex magic, are they, even though there might be a connection to you through Miss Chapman?

CROWLEY. The Ripper murders would be using a completely different system of objectification. They would be what used to be called 'black' magic.

MME POITIER. Until you came along, with a new kind.

CROWLEY. Not even new. I synthesized a number of sources of esoteric knowledge to prepare for their disclosure in the century of the common man.

MME POITIER. Will you teach me about sex magic?

CROWLEY. It's what I will do with this old bag upstairs to get her money.

MME POITIER. Oh, surely it's more than being a gigolo.

CROWLEY. It's for the creation of anything you want.

MME POITIER. So—sex magic stands in the same relationship to conventional magic as fundamentalism to the Catholic Church?

CROWLEY. Precisely, direct access.

MME POITIER. I thought magic was to do with consecrated talismans and the right objects, tongue of newt and so forth.

CROWLEY. It does, but sex magic considerably simplifies the process. The magician has a magical helper, a man or a woman and in this way, the magical current is produced. Disciplined will is important. Then there's the operation of the eighth degree, a solitary sex magical operation which if successful will produce the scarlet woman as your constant and visible companion.

MME POITIER. In other words, you bring yourself off, and you **imagine**.

CROWLEY. Yes. *(MME POITIER laughs.)*

MME POITIER. Mr Crowley, I am not a policeman, but. . . You killed someone on purpose, haven't you?

CROWLEY. He asked me to.

MME POITIER. Who was he?

CROWLEY. I can't disclose his name.

MME POITIER. I'll tell you the names of seven people I killed, if you'll teach me about sex magic.

CROWLEY *(impressed)*. Seven?

MME POITIER. Martha Turner, Mary Ann Nichols, Annie Chapman, Elisabeth Stride, Katherine Eddison, the unrecorded murder of Ruth Potter, and on the ninth of November, long after the grape harvest finished, Marie Genette Kelly.

CROWLEY. You!

MME POITIER *(dimpling)*. Enchantée. . . It was a triumph of instinct.
The first one was almost an accident, then in reading up this unusual
behaviour I found the means to power in my grasp. At any rate,
it seems to have worked. . .

CROWLEY. What did you do? How did you use the supreme
magical power?

MME POITIER. I knew I would end up like the whores if I didn't do
something about my life.

CROWLEY. What did you do?

MME POITIER *(secret smile)*. Made myself a great hotelier.

CROWLEY. What!

MME POITIER. Many people have done far worse things than
murder seven whores to get where they are. And I'm glad to
say, this hotel is better than many of its kind. I'm not boasting.
But, you will know much more about sex magic than me.

CROWLEY. You must be able to do conjurations.

MME POITIER. Pardon?

CROWLEY. Conjurations. You know, like Faustus conjuring up
Helen of Troy.

MME POITIER. You must forgive me my ignorance, but I started
rather low down in the scullery and I haven't had time to catch up.
Who is this Helen of Troy?

CROWLEY. It doesn't matter. He conjures her up, just to give the
students a look, at this famous beautiful queen.

MME POITIER. Is that wrong?

CROWLEY. No! It just doesn't go far enough. He should have
fucked her. Used her as his scarlet woman. It produces enormous
magical power. The manifestation of Helen of Troy becomes your
scarlet woman. You'd be quite impregnable, magically, if you could
keep her around.

MME POITIER. Laria is your manifestation?

CROWLEY. Laria, unfortunately, is merely human. When I was in
New York I used to strive frequently on my own for a scarlet
woman, but only get shadowy arms or legs. Once, a whole yoni
materialized briefly.

MME POITIER. Yoni?

CROWLEY. Er—vagina.

MME POITIER. Whose was it?

CROWLEY. Nobody's. It was unattached.

POITIER *(laughs politely)*. I am so stupid. I didn't know any of this.

CROWLEY. You can make manifestations?

MME POITIER. Oh yes, but I never thought to try sex magic with
them.

CROWLEY. How many people can you do?

MME POITIER. How many would you like?

CROWLEY. Amazing!

MME POITIER. Tell me some more about sex magic.

CROWLEY. No! You tell **me**. What do you do with your power?

MME POITIER. Well, some people go to the Costa Brava for their holidays, every year after we close for the winter; I rebuild London in 1888 and pass into my own creation and murder seven whores.

CRAWLEY. So you conjure a whole city?

MME. POITIER. Pas de problème . . .

CROWLEY. Well, you'll hardly need any help form me

MME POITIER. I do! Teach me about sex magic.

CROWLEY. What do I get?

MME POITIER. Anything you want.

CROWLEY. London in 1895.

MME POITIER. It will be a pleasure. Whereabouts?

CROWLEY. The Fullham Road. The moment when I chucked Willie Yeats out of the Order of the Golden Dawn's Temple for fraud. *(The lights go down.)*

MME POITIER. William Butler Yeats?

CROWLEY. Yes. He wasn't an adept, just playing around with elementals and automatic writing. A bad poet, and bog Irish. In the Fulham Road.

MME POITIER. Oh, I can find him easily. He's not there. You misremember.

CROWLEY. Is he somewhere else?

MME POITIER. He's saying goodbye to his girlfriend at the railway station—Victoria Station. Look!

*Lights vertically on MAUD GONNE and YEATS. MAUD, a tall girl with fair reddish hair, long dress surrounded by bird cages, bonnet. YEATS, long cloak, baggy trousers, sombrero.
The noise and babble of a railway station surround them, but amplified, distorted, as if twisted by the effort of recall.
Nevertheless, it is a magical effect.
CROWLEY laughs and claps his hands.*

MME POITIER. Not bad, eh? What's the girl?

CROWLEY. Maud Gonne. Fenian. She's English like so many Irish revolutionaries. *(The noise level reduces.)*

GONNE *(oblivious)*. No, Willie, I will not go with you to the Temple. It is no more than self deluding freemasonry which is the mainstay of the British Empire, to spend your time mumbling round a table with the English in a 'secret' society everyone knows about. You should be where societies have to be secret to survive; you should be in Dublin making bombs.

YEATS. I am a poet, not a plainclothes sapper. I must ask you

only to consider carefully what you would do. In the present
situation, the murder of Englishmen accomplishes nothing more
than a boast of bloody lawlessness for half an hour. But I
swear to you that if you withdraw from this I will write great
Irish national poetry.

CROWLEY. I know she's your manifestation, but. . . could I
try something with the girl?

MME POITIER. Of course. *(CROWLEY tries to undress* MAUD
GONNE *from the back. But every time he tries it, there is an
electrical crackle, and he recoils, shocked.* |MAUD *in tableau.)*
What are you doing? I'm not surprised she treats you like that.
You didn't introduce yourself.

CROWLEY. The disciplined will of the magician breaks through
to another time. . .

MME POITIER. Your rhythms are wrong. Wait a little, then join
in the conversation as if you had just passed by. *(MME POITIER
indicates a point on the floor inside which the manifestation is
taking place.)* Step close. Be still and they will shortly be able
to see you. Before, you were no more than the breeze.
(CROWLEY steps in and waits.) That's right. *(CROWLEY is
finding it difficult.)*

YEATS. I am just as sensible of the need for heroes as you.

GONNE. But not of the need to stand up and be counted. When
I talk with you of Ireland, I feel quite alone.

YEATS. I hang on your every word. I would die for a look,
a kiss—

GONNE. If you really had a tendancy to excess, you might be
a better poet.

CROWLEY. Quite right.

GONNE. You exclaim with delight for hours over Blake's
theories of London districts allocated to the human faculties,
but you do not think for a blind second of the bloody feet of
the British Empire planted in Dublin.

YEATS. Take care. Be reasonable.

GONNE. That is enough, Willie. I must go. The train is already
late. *(She exits quickly.)*

CROWLEY. Bring her on again.

MME POITER. Too late! She's caught the train!

Noises of train starting, enormous, strange, fades rapidly.
CROWLEY *stands and confronts* YEATS.

CROWLEY. Hello, Willie. *(Slowly)*

YEATS *(even)*. Crowley. *(He peers)* You look—**older**, somehow.

CROWLEY. Read my poems? *(To* |MME POITIER*)* The fraudulent
windbag.

YEATS. I have. I do not carry them with me, but I have.

CROWLEY *(to* MME POITIER*)*. He's boiling with envy. *(To* YEATS*)*

And what d'you think of them, eh? My poems. . .*(Pause)*

YEATS.   There are two lines of poetry. *(Pause)* In a porter
barrel of inconsequential verse. *(Turns)*

CROWLEY *kicks his arse so he falls over.*
YEATS *stands and turns again with a slow dignity.*

YEATS *(stately vituperation).*   You brass necked hooligan. You
are a stranger to any disciplined application of talent, should
you possess it, which I doubt. *(He turns and* CROWLEY *kicks
him again. He picks himself up.)* Your talent, I now perceive,
is as accidental as the shape of my snot; might I suggest you
join a circus *(He disappears. Lights to normal. Sound effects
go.)*

MME POITIER *(false sympathy).*   What a cheek that man has!
I did not realize you were a poet as well, and I was summoning
a professional rival. *(She gives him brandy.)*

CROWLEY.   It doesn't matter. We ought to consummate now.

MME POITIER.   Oh, but my dear Mr Crowley, I am not exactly
in the first flush of youth. . . just **tell** me about it.

CROWLEY.   Why?

MME POITIER.   I'm not sexually active, you understand. You
would have me at a disadvantage with your little games.
*(*CROWLEY *shrugs)* You see, from what you've said, I would
think that you used unstable women as your battering ram to
the astral plane. You use them up. People round you kill
each other and go mad. I find your energy intimidating. I think
you would need to crush, to dominate me. You use women.
Without them, you'd be nothing.

CROWLEY.   It's not true. Frequently I perform acts with men.
I abase myself and make myself up to play the woman.

MME POITIER.   Same problem. That's just a typical saxon
bully's sentimental whoredom. How would you react to
someone whom you found to be genuinely superior?

CROWLEY.   You! Superior! You have power, yes. But no real
knowledge.

MME POITIER.   Yes. . . I am amazed than an Ipsissimus should
be so thrown by a few anecdotes as it were, on the astral
plane. You should know our relative positions. I am above you.

CROWLEY.   . . . No, you're not!

MME POITIER.   Do you now have any power at **all**? There's nothing
wrong with your wand, is there?

CROWLEY.   What?

MME POITIER.   There's nothing the trouble with your wand. You
haven't had trouble getting an erection?

CROWLEY.   No. The one problem I do have is my orgasm is
holding back.

MME POITIER.   What have you been doing about this?

CROWLEY. Opium, ether, laudanum, cocaine, heroin, the
   occasional flask of wine. I can tolerate opium very well. I have
   a great deal in common with the Chinese. It's heroin which is
   the bad boy. It makes me go deaf.
MME POITIER. Why don't you retire to a job? It doesn't hurt.
CROWELY *(softly)*. It is written, it is the destiny of Alastor,
   the Wanderer of the Waste. . .

LARIA *comes in. She is dressed in* DIDEROT'S *clothes. She is
stoned. She goes behind* CROWLEY.

MME POITIER. I like your friend. The scarlet woman.
CROWLEY. Laria? Oh, yes.
MME POITIER. Couldn't you do it with her, and I could watch?
CROWLEY. I doubt if you'd see anything unusual.
MME POITIER. I might. If there is this campaign against you in
   the press, why are you both going back to England? If you're
   broke and you've failed, they'll only pour more abuse on your
   heads. Are you gluttons for punishment? *(DIDEROT enters
   minus his uniform, clad only in a white towel. He is stern-
   faced.)*
CROWLEY. I didn't know we were going back. I thought we
   were still under arrest.

LARIA *finds* DIDEROT'S *gun and gets it out of the holster and
points it at* DIDEROT *who shrugs and raises his hands perfunct-
orily.*

LARIA. Not any more. Beast, let's get out of here!
CROWLEY. Not yet. We have unfinished business. How did
   all this start? *(Cool)*
LARIA. He wanted me to beat him with me wearing his uniform.
MME POITIER. Is that sex magic?
LARIA. Not unless you feel strongly about policemen. It's
   the price of freedom.
MME POITIER. And you would do it?
LARIA. Do it? I should have got the gun out and killed him!
   Bastard!
CROWLEY *(mildly)*. Do what thou wilt shall be all the law.
   (LARIA sings snatches from 'Ten Cents a Dance',)
LARIA. Ten cents a dance, that's what they pay me, gosh how
   they weigh me down.
MME. POITIER. Tell me about Laria.
CROWLEY. She's a whore, a scarlet whore, a woman in a million.
   I'd be lost without her.
MME POITIER. And you had a child?
CROWLEY. Yes, we did. Once.
MME POITIER. She looks tired. Why don't you come and sit
   down for a bit, Laria?

LARIA. D'you mind if I interrupt the great work for a few minutes?

MME POITIER. Oh! We're not . . . going that way.

LARIA. That's what they all say. Isn't it? *(Gun in* CROWLEY'S *ear)* but one little sniff at beauty boy here, and religion, law, marriage come tumbling down. He loves to see it tumbling down. We're catalysts. People realize their true nature through us, and that sets them free. Free hotels, free policemen, lust and love both exist, both are separate, both are free. Aren't they, old Prick?

CROWLEY. What?

LARIA. **Lust and love and hate and everything else exist but it's all free.**

CROWLEY. Oh. Yes. *(*LARIA *pokes the gun at* CROWLEY, *who tries not to react.)*

LARIA. I could have saved myself a whole lot of trouble. I could have filled Old Prick here full of holes. I didn't think of that. *(Sticks her face in* CROWLEY'S *and puts the gun to his head.)* Remember my **face**. . . Remember my face. . . It's the last thing you're going to **see**. *(To* MME POITIER*)* Old Prick has a rather rudimentary grasp of people's faces. That's why when he fucks somebody else he can still think it's **me**.

MME POITIER. What is it exactly that you do together that is so special?

LARIA. He does all the work. I just lie there with my legs open. *(Taunting* CROWLEY*)* The work involves cleansing of the sexual wound. *(Arch.)* But when he took the wrapping off to clean it, poor Beast was mistaken for one of the maggots.

CROWLEY. Don't be stupid. *(*LARIA *puts gun in* CROWLEY'S *face again.)*

LARIA. And we exterminate maggots, especially when they appear disguised as bald apes with hardons. Yes, **you**. *(Sings)* 'Ten cents a dance, that's what they pay me, Gosh how they weigh me down. Ten cents a dance, pansies and rough guys, Touch guys who tear my gown. . .' *(She sprawls amiably in a chair. She holds out her hand and watches it minutely.)* I'm starting to fade. The Scarlet woman is starting to fade . . . what colour will she go? I need a little snort to bring the colour back into my cheeks. *(Turns to the other two)* And what have you two done this evening? Kept the black dog off your back, have you? *(To* CROWLEY*)* Had any good sex magic lately?

CROWLEY. Madame Poitier is interested in . . . the occult.

LARIA *(sings)*. Tinkers and tailors and one-legged sailors can pay for a ticket and rent me. . . Butchers and bakers, and rats from the harbours. . .

CROWLEY. She has considerable experience, but none at all

when it comes to the left hand way.

LARIA. Oh yeah?

CROWLEY. She wants to learn about sex magic, Laria.

LARIA *(mimic)*. 'She wants to learn about sex magic, Laria.'
Well . . . darling, it's like this. If you want something, you use
your whole personality, your whole sexuality, to bring about
its creation. It's as easy as falling off a log. and it should catch
on like wild fire. I am to perform an act of sex magic with the
repulsive Mr Diderot, in order to secure our freedom. Sex magic
has nothing to do with normal attraction; in fact the more
prejudices you overcome, the better the outcome will be.
Health, Strength, Freedom. . . I am going to diddle Diderot for
our freedom, freedom, freedom! Otherwise, we may be cast into
the innermost dungeons with little pink-eyed ratssss. . . If you
like, you can watch.

MME POITIER. Thank you. I've been trying to get Mr Crowley
to show me all evening. How long have you been practising?

LARIA. Oh, years . . . you may think that you see a pair of
emotionally and financially bankrupt junkies, vilified beyond
their wildest dreams in the press—but no! We're on the road to
freedom. Even if we weren't, the law is not affected. So What
Thou Wilt shall be the whole of the Law. *(The phone rings.)*
It's for you. *(*MME POITIER *picks it up.)* I am above the world,
watching, time and space . . . are irritations . . . continuity? . . .
pooh . . . the **power** is given to us by the secret chiefs . . . from
sex magic.

MME POITIER *(simultaneously)*. Ah bon . . . ah bon . . . je lui
dirai . . . merci, Madame. *(Phone down. To* CROWLEY*)* She
will see you now.

CROWLEY. Who?

MME POITIER. The woman upstairs.

CROWLEY *(to* MME POITIER*)*. Do you think I could have
something to raise the ecstatic current?

MME POITIER. But you've already had almost a bottle of brandy.

CROWLEY. I am not really affected by alcohol, but if there were
some ether . . . you can see very deeply into things . . . sometimes
so deeply you can't even make connections . . . if I had some
ether. . .

MME POITIER. But you can't go and see her **drugged**.

CROWLEY. Why not?

MME POITIER. She won't see you!

CROWLEY. How do you know!

MME POITIER. I couldn't allow it in my hotel. Suppose something
happened?

CROWLEY. The whole idea is to get something to happen.

MME POITIER. Yes, but what? I retired from magic before your
scientific breakthrough, but I seem to be in better condition for

practising it than you. I can do it alone. What would you be if
I took your Scarlet Woman away?

CROWLEY. You! You're just a stack of invoices. There are a
million fakers like you. A few card tricks up your sleeve and
you think you're a secret chief. The one definite test of a magus
is that they are held without honour in their own country, and
that test I fulfill.

MME POITIER. I would pass that test for a magus. No one here
knows my other status.

CROWLEY *(coldly)*. So what do you want to know?

MME POITIER. Can you do anything, or is it all a tall story?

CROWLEY. It's got to be a tall story, really, hasn't it? Like the
Ripper being an adept is a tall story. Could you bring the heroin?
I have to get to work. *(POITIER is about to phone, but then
stops.)*

MME. POITIER. I'd heard so much about you. I was so pleased when
you came. I thought, here is one man in the whole world who would
understand me. And you don't understand me, and you don't understand history either. If you don't understand what makes people
tick, what's the point of trying to start a religion?

CROWLEY. Of course I understand you. I feel as if at Cefalu I've
been trying to run a second rate resort for the last year. In the
end, there is really very little difference between us.

MME. POITIER. You are a fraud. You let lies about yourself blow
about the world. You do not act from your centre. You have no
centre. You have no heart. I do. I also serve. I am of convenience and
help to weary travellers. The first act of life is an act of violence, and
we spend the rest of our time on earth making up for it.

When I killed, it was with eyes averted. I have always been prudish,
I can tell you. As for the consumption of pudenda, I was sick. But
you nothing revolts, nothing distresses. You are a monster who preys
on the weak or is preyed upon without scruple, without regret, a
lover of power and unmasked violence, the sneer on the face of the
dinosaur, a pathetic and dangerous desire to shock, but finally a
fraud, a drug fiend, a would-be magician who has forgotten the
invocations and relies on impressing his supporters with his
sexual prowess.

Sooner or later, Crowley, it all comes home to roost. Sooner or later,
we all discover who we are. You have been so negligent of your
personality that you stand no more chance of integrity than a man
with asthma trying to blow up a burst paper bag. Civilisation is
infinitely more dangerous than anything that you have indulged in.

You do not wish to understand the great struggles that tear us apart.
You wish only to discard in favour of your shabby Egyptology. You
are a man without awareness of yourself or your past, a man of

unconscious cruelty; a child who has dabbled in what he believes to be magic, who cozens the credulous into belief because of his blind voyaging into areas where anyone would lose their soul, except this deaf rotting hulk.

Who do you serve, except the forces of chaos in this rotten world? Yes, I'll get you your drugs so you can go upstairs, and I hope never see you again. *(Phone)* Demandez à Monsieur Diderot qu'il apporte l'héroine.

LARIA.   Where does he get it?

MME POITIER.   He's a police chief, isn't he?

LARIA.   How come he's got this funny hard patch on his stomach?

MME POITIER.   He uses heroin. At his desk in the prefecture, he has a drawer, with a syringe with a weak solution in it. In meetings which sometimes go on for eight hours, he leans forward as if to get something out . . . and injects himself in the stomach. It's because the job's so dull. *(DIDEROT comes in with towel and heroin.)*

LARIA.   You a magician? What grade?

MME POITIER.   I'm retired. *(CROWLEY takes heroin and injects.)*

LARIA.   What are you going upstairs for. Beast?

CROWLEY.   A magical working. There's a woman.

LARIA.   But I was up there with Diderot. There's nobody there. I looked in every room.

CROWLEY.   Madame Poitier assured me that there was. It's conceivable that she could be wrong. Or is it?

LARIA.   Who's your guardian? How d'you summon them?

MME POITIER.   I don't have one. I look after myself.

LARIA.   Don't you have to have one to protect you if something goes wrong in a manifestation?

MME POITIER.   Nothing every does go wrong.

CROWLEY.   This certainly is a weak solution. *(Finishes injecting)* Before I go upstairs, I would like to show Madame Poitier something. Just Madame Poitier. Everyone else out.

DIDEROT.   But I wanted to see a trick!

CROWLEY.   Everyone but Madame Poitier out. *(To LARIA)* You, too.

MME POITIER.   We're going to be all by ourselves, eh?

DIDEROT *and* LARIA *exit.*
Music. Incantatory, throbbing. Lights change.
POITIER *is half amused, half frightened by the display.*

MME POITIER.   How skilful, Mr Crowley! *(Disarmingly)* It reminds me of something I saw at the Opera-Comique, on my first honeymoon. . . *(Pause)* Is this, tell me, sex magic? Or is it just fireworks? *(POITIER suddenly starts.)* Ah! Just a moment, there is something crawling round inside my skirt. *(CROWLEY watching her from the table, making it happen. She is paralysed with fear.)* Is it a mouse?

I don't want it inside me. It's hard! Ah! It's a **knife!** *(She starts sobbing hysterically.)* Don't cut me there, please have pity. *(She is completely under* CROWLEY'S *spell.)*

CROWLEY.   I'm going to do to you what you did to the seven whores.

MME POITIER.   Don't cut it out, don't cut it, please.

CROWLEY *(inquisitorial).*   Why is there no woman upstairs?

MME POITIER *(sobbing).*   I don't know, I don't know. Take that badness out of me, please. Don't cut me.

CROWLEY.   Drink my seed.

MME POITIER.   No! That's **dirty!** *(*MME POITIER *is vanquished.)*

CROWLEY.   If you don't want to be too close to the fountain head, you could eat my shit.

POITER *is weeping hysterically. The encounter is over and he has won this time.*
The lights and the sound go back to normal.
MME POITIER *picks herself up, sniffing.*

CROWLEY.   So you were the woman upstairs.

MME POITIER *(pious).*   I was going to give you a wonderful time. I was going to appear before you. I was going to refurbish the rooms as they were before the war when the Prince Regent used to stay here. And you would have taught me sex magic in his bed.

CROWLEY.   So why did you refuse me down here?

MME POITIER.   I wanted to be loved.

DIDEROT *enters.* POITIER *pulls herself together. Flashing them both a dirty look,* POITIER *exits.* DIDEROT *smiles.*
DIDEROT.   So, how are you getting on with Madame Poitier?

CROWLEY.   Oh, fine.

DIDEROT.   She likes the girls, you know? Prefers them to . . . *(He pokes his forefinger through a ring he makes with the other forefinger and thumb.)* She tells me very little. But meanwhile, while we are waiting. . . M'sieur, I have a problem. *(He indicates box.)*

CROWLEY.   Is that for me?

DIDEROT.   I am not very far advanced in magic.

CROWLEY.   How far?

DIDEROT.   Very little.

CROWLEY.   D'you know the Cabala?

DIDEROT.   No.

CROWLEY.   Clairvoyancy? Clairaudiency?

DIDEROT.   No—it's a simple problem.

CROWLEY.   Who's your holy guardian angel?

DIDEROT.   I dunno.

CROWLEY.   What are the watchtowers?

46

DIDEROT.   On the corners of large prisons—

CROWLEY.   On the astral plane. Can you become invisible?

DIDEROT.   You mistake me. I can be inconspicuous—I am inconspicuous—but it's magic I want to know. Animal tricks. My wife is a magician, but she won't show me. *(He produces a very small top hat, and a very large stuffed rabbit. Puts them both on the table.)* How is it done? How would you make the rabbit disappear, eh?

CROWLEY.   I've no idea.

DIDEROT.   M'sieur, a poor policeman who wants to learn a few simple tricks to amuse the orphanage. . .

CROWLEY.   Shut your eyes. *(DIDEROT shuts them. CROWLEY puts the rabbit under the table, turns the hat over, puts his finger on the hat to prevent DIDEROT looking under it.)* Open your eyes. You see, to make magic serve worldly interests like you want, is a perversion of its true nature, which stands outside social success completely. Have you tried incest?

DIDEROT.   No, not recently. Why?

CROWLEY.   Incest is the way which the Egyptian Royal lines used to keep the magical power in the family.

DIDEROT.   Would it make me more popular?

CROWLEY.   Have you a sister?

DIDEROT.   She's forty eight.

CROWLEY.   Just the right age. ·

DIDEROT.   My wife has a weak heart. She would die if she found out.

CROWLEY.   How could she if you didn't tell her?

DIDEROT.   I don't know. But she does.| *(Whispers)* She told me Madame Poitier *(draws his finger across his throat)* more than once.

CROWLEY.   Have you seen her doing it?

DIDEROT.   No.

CROWLEY.   Do you have evidence?

Interested, CROWLEY *takes finger off hat.* DIDEROT *immediately turns it over to find it empty.*

DIDEROT *(philosophically).*   Exactly, Mr Crowley, where is the evidence? *(CROWLEY puts the rabbit back on the table.* DIDEROT *suspicious again.)* Can you really do magic?

CROWLEY.   There was a magus in the Far East in the eighth century. He was an adept and had mastered the Indian rope trick. This means, that by arcane forces, the adept balances a large ball of sisal rope on his fist with one finger holding it in place, then hurls it vertically into the sky where it unravels and finally disappears from sight, leaving one end dangling.

DIDEROT.   Yes?

CROWLEY.   A ruler demanded to see this and the adept was forced to show him on pain of death. The ruler, much delighted with the display, commanded his young son to climb up the rope. The son did and was soon lost to sight. An hour later, his trunkless head, severed limbs and body fell to the desert.

DIDEROT. Well?

CROWLEY. Look on my works, ye mighty, and despair. *(Pause)* Magic is dangerous.

DIDEROT. Show me something and I'll let you go.

CROWLEY. What do you want to know?

DIDEROT. A trick.

CROWLEY. Life is a trick.

DIDEROT. Show me, please.

CROWLEY. I would have to show you the separation of the body and soul.

DIDEROT. And why is that a trick?

CROWLEY. The disembodied spirit is offered the phantom feast of the material world, and falls for it, till death rescues it. Where's Laria?

DIDEROT. I'm sure Madam Poitier will look after her. Show me this **death**, then.

CROWLEY *doesn't answer. A wind begins to blow and the lights start to change instead. Music.* CROWLEY *flexes his arms in an incantation, informally, like a sumo wrestler. Then he stops.* DIDEROT *is fascinated.*

DIDEROT. Please, continue. Laria is qute safe. I am sure they are just talking.

The lights go down to a spot on DIDEROT'S *face as he 'sees' what* CROWLEY *describes. Musical chanting mixes in with the wind.*

CROWLEY. Death touched me once on Kanjenchunga, in the form of the spirit of the five peaks. I felt his breath on my beard.

(To DIDEROT*)* To see death, plain, you have to be invisible. You're becoming invisible.

DIDEROT *(prosaic).* I'm becoming invisible.

CROWLEY. Watch your body flicker, waver then disappear. The eyes remain. Two pools of dark. Then they too disappear. You are on the astral plane. North, South, East, West, time doesn't exist, only what you make of them. You are a spectator of the spectacle of the demon of the five peaks.

DIDEROT. Five peaks.

CROWLEY *(behind).* You are invisible in another plane. Before you, the spirit of Kanchenjunga, the spirit of the five peaks. See him. He sees you. The irreducible five in one: from the five, nine glaciers, from the glaciers, fifty rivers, from the rivers a million rhododendrons, wrapped in leeches and shrill clouds.

Ice falls, snow breaks from the ridge.

No footholds in falling ice. The clouds tie the summit in the icy
dark. The ice brushes men off like wingless flies. Bind nothing.
Let there be no division. All is sacrifice. All entities points of
light in the eternal dark. The leeches toil. The men fall. The ice
gorge opens, and four men are locked in the ice. Home at last.
Four men dead. Number five. Number five. *(Effects conclude,
lights to normal.)*

DIDEROT *(cool, interested).*   I saw! Well done! It was dusk—the
porters fell down the crevasse—and you were responsible for
that debacle? I am very impressed. No . . . moved. I was even
for a moment frightened. That was quite outstanding. It cut to
the heart of the matter, as my wife says. She's a magician too,
did you know? Welcome to our humble abode.

CROWLEY.   Thank you, commissioner, but it's time we were
going; we have to catch that boat.

DIDEROT.   Two years ago I married Madame Poitier.

CROWLEY *(tired).*   Congratulations.

DIDEROT.   She doesn't want me to touch her. In the time of
the marriage, I have been six hundred and sixty six times to
the brothel. And yet, I love her. She admires you.

CROWLEY.   She's jealous.

DIDEROT.   Don't you think it strange, that someone like her
should want to marry a poor policeman? I'm so sorry I'm
keeping you talking when you want to get aboard the boat.
I'd like to give you something to take with you though. We
have some refined opium which we impounded from a Chinese
freighter. Come *(*DIDEROT *waves the passports enticingly in
front of the tired* CROWLEY.*)* Life in Sicily must have been
paradise. I envy you in the creation of a new world religion.
What a pity the fascists threw your brave example out. Come.
(They eixt.)

The MAITRE D' *comes on to the 'UPSTAIRS', repositioning a
table and bringing a cheval mirror. Music begins immediately*
DIDEROT *finishes.* MME POITIER *and* LARIA *enter as the*
MAITRE D' *concludes and exits.*

MME POITIER.   What's that between your breasts?

LARIA.   The mark of the Beast.

MME POITIER *(to herself).*   Salope. Cheap jewelery. Filth.

LARIA.   The Scarlet Woman must be loud and adulterous and
wear finery.

MME POITIER.   Doesn't sex magic say anything about washing?

LARIA.   No. This is a magical working. The dirt is symbolic of
the earth.

MME POITIER.   You've practically no breasts.

LARIA.   Look at my essence. The uglier, the unhappier, the better, the more the true nature is revealed. Glorify the great whoredom and we shall become free. The law is do what thou wilt. You will play the man.

MME POITIER.   Turn around. Head back. *(She produces a flick knife. The police chief enters.)*

DIDEROT.   Hey—Madame Poitier! *(MME POITER slowly puts the knife down.)* J'ai vu—un grand montage—là bas! Il est pas mal—quoi?

LARIA.   Two is better than one, a magical act. We will invoke Choronozon. You will take me from the front, and you in the mouth. This is an act which invariably secures freedom.

DIDEROT.   Sex magic, yes?

LARIA.   We invoke—freedom. I'd like some brandy. We invoke the Law.

MME POITIER *(to DIDEROT)*.   Get her a brandy. You can have her when I've finished. *(LARIA sits frontstage DIDEROT exits.)*

LARIA.   I'm so tired.

MME POITIER.   Kick off your shoes.

LARIA.   I'm so tired. I sometimes feel. . . I sometimes feel that . . . the difference between being free and not being free is so small that you can't see. You might just as well not bother. *(The MAITRE D' hands MME POITIER a pair of lighted candles which she places downstage of the table.)* And sometimes I can't remember the words of the great work. And it's all so much harder, when you've got thrush, and gonorrhea, and crabs. . . I sometimes wonder why some of us are just tessellated pricks, and the rest of us are tessellated cunts . . . the latter being a special sort of punishment for those whose ambition it is to surpass themselves. The receiving. The earth. All those passive bits in the I Ching. The dark, quiet bit. Surpass yourself, he says, bring yourself up to my level. I can be passive and womanly. I can lay around the left bank waiting for stokers on leave. Teach them the law. Stoke what though wilt. Stoke the little children away. Their little smiles, little rosebud lips, flaming up the chimney, so it rains smiles. Reach out for the active bit, standing on someone.

Humiliation. Power. But he's alright, but I did cry, when it turned out it was the kids' turn to die. I did cry a bit then, but it's stupid, really, to cry because it's all in the great plan. I'm a pile of liver in the corner, with a hauntingly beautiful mouth . . . my soul is a star.

But to know you're dead before you start, to come into the first bleeding round, crying. . . Look! Liver lips . . . crying! And my first period my mother wouldn't touch me. I thought I was dying.

The curse comes from the other people. The Beast lifts the curse.

Everything is equal, before the great work. I was nothing before he found me. A dead star. When I leave him, I'll be nothing again. If you think blood and spunk is the ultimate experience, you're right. That's when it all happens. The rest is . . . the other side of the moon.

And is she going to kill me? I'm fully protected . . . I don't care. I think that I despise the human race a bit less from where I am. than from any other place. . . But why do there have to be opposites—Scarlet Woman and the Beast, the cruel and the meek. Why don't we all be Beasts, and beat each other? Nobody ever said why . . . Why we couldn't all be Beasts. *(MME POITIER comes forward and starts to wash her feet.)*

Perhaps it's an additional refinement to the magical future of the world. Who taught the Beast how to be the Beast? Was it in his nature?

Naar . . . it was in his upbringing, wasn't it? All he did was turn it upside down, and watch the worms dancing in the sunlight. And then clean, clean, clean. Everyone is clean, everyone's a star. Are you going to kill me? You could get away with it.

MME POITIER. I'll try to be good to you. But I have to be boss.

LARIA. You can't guarantee anything. You can't make bargains. You can't trade in human flesh like the rest of the world. I couldn't make bargains with the secret chiefs to make my child stay alive, so I didn't try. . . Either they want you, or they don't. The rest is . . . just life, but sometimes the colours were so bright you'd think you were flying. I am the Scarlet Woman.

MME POITIER. Of course. I'm interested in your power. You're the channel for the power of the Beast.

LARIA. Yeah, a lot of power. Not cheap tricks for the crowd, but the incarnation of a being, glorious, timeless, stretching back aeons. Bring in the new aeon, with its hail of blood. I really **mean** something in the universe. And what I **do** means something. I mean, I write them down in my diary, all my magical acts.

Health. Sanity. Freedom. Beast says, musn't be afraid of madness. Musn't be afraid of going over the edge. What edge? We're all in space. We're all planets, whirling round and round, blazing trails of glory in the dark. I'm not like the other scarlet women he had. Second-rate bloody women. Gloria! Read Gloria's magic diary. I did once, and not one thing in it that I couldn't have down twice as well.

There's only one Beast, One Logos of the Aeon, and I'm his Scarlet Woman. The interpreter of the book of the law. Nothing can unite the divided unless it's love. Everything else is just the fuel. Lust. Hate. Fuel for the scarlet woman to burn in the heart. *(Stands)*

If you're the scarlet woman—you got to be proud! You got to be wicked in front of everybody—don't hold anything back. Steal from the poor, kill the rich. Such the enemies' blood! Yes, that's very, very good! *(The lighting has shrunk down to a murky, murderous gloom.* MME POITIER'S *knife gleams in the dark.)*

Go on, then. Kill me. I'm ready. Beast would like that. I'm a millstone round his neck. Go on, you've done this before, haven't you. Quite a dab hand at killing your own sex. You've made a pile of money out of saying "no" to people. I think all these people who say yes to everything like me, they must be quite a threat. Go on, I dare you. Kill me. Let's see where your polite behaviour stops. *(MME POITIER makes a feeble and genteel stab at* LARIA. LARIA *knocks the knife away and it falls on the floor.)*

You can't deal with real passion, can you? Yours is all fake. You've squeezed it back till it died. I was ready to die for him, and you fucked it up. You miserable, dried up old cunt. You've been fantasising for fifty years and now when it comes to the point, you can't do it in real life at all!

Riddled with confusion and guilt, MME POITIER *totters to the back and turns on a light switch. The lights go bright.* DIDEROT *is visible at the back, unobtrusive as always. Alert and attentive.*

LARIA *(satisfied)*. He got to you in the end, didn't he. *(Confidential)* Isn't he a bastard.

MME POITIER. Yes, he hurt me inside. . . He was rough . . . I had done nothing to offend him. . . I was impotent in front of his rudeness. I am sorry. I thought to take it out on you. I am too old for this. I should not have become angry with him. I did not want him in the way he wanted me. You see, he destroys his women.

LARIA. Well, what did you do with yours? Did anyone put them back together again? You're no better than he is.

MME POITIER *(serious)*. I did **repent**. *(LARIA laughs coarsely.)* Laria, have you ever thought of a separate existence?

LARIA *(relaxed)*. From the Beast? No, I'm his Scarlet Woman.

MME POITIER. Only for as long as you want to be. .

LARIA. Are you offering me a job?

MME POITIER. No.

LARIA. Well, what then? *(MME POITIER takes a silken rope from* DIDEROT.*)*

MME POITIER. This rope is life. *(Tugs at it)* Feel it! **Strong**. . . Some people are tightrope walkers, and some people prefer to have themselves tied up. If you stay with this man, you will be tied up.

LARIA. But if I left him, I wouldn't be a scarlet woman anymore.

MME POITIER. Why not?

LARIA. I'd be nobody. I couldn't leave him.

MME. POITIER. Very well. We will raise the stakes. That is the door to the quay, and that is the door to the railway station. *(Points.)* If you choose the railway station, I will give you a ticket to wherever you want to go. If you choose to go to the quay with Mr Crowley, we will let you go, but first, you will have unfinished business with the commissioner. I'm not sure what. Something they don't allow him to do to the girls at the brothel.

DIDEROT *(soberly)*. Smash the face. Split the nostril. Black the eye.

MME POITIER. Laria, is it so difficult to turn away from the pain? Do you really think that if you stopped hurting, you would cease to exist?

LARIA *(triumphant in her masochism)*. What's the good of talking?

She takes DIDEROT by the hand and begins to draw him off. He turns and shrugs at MME POITIER. The MAITRE D' begins to move the table and mirror upstage for the final scene. MME POITIER weeps tears of shame and frustration.

Music ends. Lights dim downstage. Harbour noises. CROWLEY enters with suitcase. Sits on it.

LARIA makes a long slow entrance through the lamplight, toward him. Halfway there she turns and spits out some blood. CROWLEY gets up and turns away, deliberately stares out to sea. LARIA sits down unsteadily on the suitcase that he has brought out with him.

LARIA. Give me my passport.

CROWLEY. Get up. We're going to be late.

LARIA. I'm not going with you. I've had enough.

CROWLEY. Oh? Where were you thinking of going?

LARIA. America. *(pause)* Do you know why I hate you? I'm leaving you? *(Pause)* You could have stopped me being kicked and beaten up and raped by that police commissioner. You could.

CROWLEY. And so could you.

LARIA. You **do** sacrifice people. You **do** like their blood. And now I've given and given and there's nothing left to give. Why don't you go and find someone else and live off them. You just use people. Go on, fuck off. There are plenty of women stupid enough to let people like you walk all over them. I'm leaving you, understand? You left me in that shithole, for them to do what they liked with me, and you didn't care a shit about little Binky. You don't care so I'm leaving you. I doubt if you'd care about that much either. *(Arch)* It doesn't affect the law of 'Do what

thou Wilt.' *(CROWLEY takes a passport out of his jacket.)*
CROWLEY *(checking).*   This is your passport. . .

LARIA *holds up her hand for it and* CROWLEY *throws it off stage.*

LARIA.   Where is it? What have you done with it?
CROWLEY.   Can you swim?
LARIA.   No.
CROWLEY.   It's in the water. Over there. *(He points* LARIA
    stands unsteadily.)
LARIA.   Why? Why did you do that?
CROWLEY.   You won't need it if you're not coming with me.
    I can always find another Scarlet Woman.
LARIA.   Wait a minute. I don't have any money.
CROWLEY.   There are plenty of sailors.
LARIA.   No thanks.
CROWLEY.   It's your decision. But if you don't save yourself,
    no one else will save you. And I'm not looking after you any
    more.
LARIA *(pointing to her bruises).*   Call that looking after me?
CROWLEY *(shrugs).*   Do what thou wilt shall be the whole
    of the Law.
LARIA *(automatically).*   Love is the Law, love under will.
    (Pause.) Well. *(She turns to go)* Goodnight.

CROWLEY *stares out at the darkened sea, sitting on the case
again.* LARIA *suddenly turns back to look at him. Music, as
at the end of ACT ONE, energetic, incantatory, then, a split
second later, blackout.*

Flaming Bodies

Flaming Bodies was first performed at the ICA on 1 December 1979. The cast was:

ROGER UNGLESS, etc.   Hugh Thomas
MERCEDES   Miriam Margolyes
IRENE, etc.   Julie Walters

Directed by John Ashford

Designed by Gemma Jackson

ACT ONE

An office in Los Angeles. Night.
MERCEDES *enters through partition door. Goes to fridge. Crosses*
to computer. Laughs at print out information. Sits in her chair.
She hears the sound of the elevator and exits through her door.
Enter ROGER *and* IRENE.

ROGER. Of course, everything here says it—but, Welcome to
California. The sun shines constantly through the smog here
and there is the most terrifying chance of actually getting what
you want, and there's only one thing worse than getting what you
want, and that's getting what you deserve, but I came here to get
on, and you've just arrived here to get on, so it must have something.

D'you want to make a lot of money? Just about everyone else in the
film business wants to, but I suppose there are exceptions. Did you
leave England thinking that all English men are shits or was it the
weather? I suppose you had some awful affairs with sensitive young
men just down from Cambridge and finding themselves. In my
experience—and of course I pissed off after my second year—the
major cultural event was these same sensitive young men coming down
from Cambridge and writing novels about sensitive young men coming
down from Cambridge and finding themselves. Curious that between
London and Cambridge—quite a short distance—so many young men
should get lost. I was always too insensitive so I just stayed in
California with a gay friend of mine and elbowed him out of his job
when he took to the booze in a big way. You don't have anything to
fear from me, I mean I won't pinch your bottom.
IRENE. Thank you.
ROGER. It's nothing. I only hope you manage to find a straight bloke.
Now, your job here. What did they tell you in London?
IRENE. Nothing.
ROGER. Nothing . . . Wow. Too much. *(nodding).* Nothing. *(pause)*
We're going to have to start from scratch. First of all Welcome.
IRENE. You've said that once already.
ROGER. I really mean it this time. *(pause)* No, what I mean is, I'm

only going to work with one story editor, and that's you. See?

IRENE. Sorry?

ROGER. This was your predecessor's office. The . . . girl I had before.
But she can't get in any more, or stay in here, not when I've got rid
of that fridge of hers. She eats, you see, continuously. She's **oral**.
As we say round here, where Freudian tautologies have found their
way into the language. Her body another circle round the engulfing
mouth. So—whoosh! I got rid of her, I thought. But there's something here—and although I haven't seen her, she stays and stays and
stays. I don't think she's in love with me—I should hope not—so
when I've got rid of the fridge . . . You look at me with those big
eyes of yours, are you an ingenue or do you know it all? Of course,
you know it all. Yes well there was something else, a disagreement
we had not just to do with her masturbating or her lesbianism. You
know about masturbating? Good. She says there's an idea here which
is hers. And I fired her to keep it. Well I said why didn't you register
it with the Screen Writers Guild you can do that if it was yours and
you know all that. Paranoia. That's the problem with these extremely
fascist left wing dykes in this country—they're into primalism. Of
course I don't have to tell you what primalism is—

IRENE. Would you?

ROGER. Involuntarily of course—they don't admit it but because they
assume the male function they're into Oedipal massacre. The men are
all their father collectively and so chop chop they want to finish them
off with a cutlet bat. Well! And she said, it was her idea that we'd make
this movie about old J.C. with a split tail or at any rate some different
plumbing. Androgene? And well she wanted to take it over make it into
some motherfucking feminist tract, brilliant girl but totally unstable—
and I said look the people with the money are seventy percent hetero,
a hundred percent conservative and a hundred percent believers in the
Bible Belt, so you're going to have to get yourself cleaned up and stay
quiet and let me write this one. All it needs is a few sentences—something not enough to make them panic and the producers will come up
with the goods. But it's got to be packaged right. Very few ideas are th
ideas of one man—let alone one mad woman. . . You think you can
cope? Just give me a hand getting rid of this fridge will you?

They unplug and glide the fridge smoothly off.
As they go off MERCEDES *walks from her room and watches their exit*
unobserved. She takes up IRENE'S *fur coat and wraps it round her like*
a blanket, then wanders back off stage as if to bed.
Re-enter ROGER *and* IRENE.
ROGER *dusting both of them down like a hairdresser.*

ROGER. It's the plane which does terrible things to skirts—they should
do free dry-cleaning I think. Anyhow that's all her clutter out of here
and so I don't expect we'll be troubled again. Thanks. I'll give you
something for that. *(Gets a huge jar of pills from the shelf.)* Put your

hands out.

IRENE *does. He fills her hands to overflowing and then they go over the floor. Millions of them.*

ROGER. Shit.

IRENE. Sorry.

ROGER. Leave them for now, clear up in the morning.

IRENE. I don't take pills. Up to now . . .

ROGER. No no no they're **garlic** pills. Garlic.

IRENE. For vampires?

ROGER. No, for health. Everybody takes them here. They're garlic, but without the smell. I take around forty a day. Your predecessor used to chew whole bulbs like a fruit. *(He holds his nose.)* Although I suppose it drowned the draught coming out of her armpits. . . Right, let's go.

IRENE. Where's my coat?

ROGER. Was it here? Oh, someone must have walked in and nicked it. Sorry. Pity.

IRENE. Well . . . *(brave)* I suppose I don't really need it now.

ROGER. Well you would have, yes, everybody wears them to work. Doesn't matter how hot it is.

IRENE. Oh damn.

ROGER. What's the matter?

IRENE. Nothing . . . I'll just check to see if I haen't left it somewhere—

ROGER. You can if you like, I'll see you in the lobby . . . No, it's gone. Shouldn't leave the door open, see . . .

Exits.

IRENE *has a brief look around for the coat then sits down and has a small strangulated weep.*

MERCEDES *comes on silently, without shoes, from behind.*

MERCEDES *(fierce).* What's the matter?

IRENE. I can't find my coat. *(MERCEDES takes it from around her waist and drapes it over* IRENE'S *shoulders.)*

MERCEDES. There's your coat, sister. *(She hears* ROGER *coming back. She exits too late.)*

ROGER. Got it? Good. *(Cuddles her in an abstracted, manipulative way.)* Come on love. Get a move on. What's all the fuss about?

IRENE *(stands brave).* I'm far from home.

ROGER. There's always the phone. *(Sniffs suspiciously.)* Fee fi, fo fum. Or am I imagining it? I'm catching the cultural disease of open paranoia. Must be.

IRENE. I'm sorry.

ROGER. Don't be sorry for showing your feelings, You see Californians of all Americans are really into their heads right? People want to talk to you about the most intimate details of your psychodrama, right? You have to talk about the inner landscape here—there's not

59

not much point in discussing the weather . . . and so you get to know everything about people.

IRENE.   That must be difficult sometimes.

ROGER.   No! There's a kind of get-out clause, invented by mother nature, to prevent overloading the circuits and merging of personalities in each other's problems. You meet someone, you become totally integrated into their life their dress what turns them on—and then you wake up one morning beside them *(exiting)* to find that you are lying next to the body of a perfectly formed but quite uninteresting stranger . . .

Exeunt IRENE *and* ROGER.
Much locking of door behind them.
Re-enter MERCEDES.

MERCEDES.   OK go ahead and nab my refrigerator. It's all part of the grand plan. The last three days, I was able to eat only during the hours of darkness—olives, potato chips, onion rings—four dozen executive snacks—half a deep frozen waffle someone had left, that was a mistake—but now part two of the diet comes into operation. You're not going to scare me out of here. I may be hungry, but I'm not afraid. *(Picks up a garlic pill.)* Maybe a few of these would staunch the cries of the mutinous organ. *(Eats a few)* Calorific value guaranteed nil . . . *(pause, takes some more)* You get to like it. Not as good as the real thing. *(takes out a twist of tails of garlic from her dress and throws it in the wastepaper basket.)* Goodnight sweet prince . . . *(tries to match up the shredded pieces of paper while eating handfuls of garlic pills)* I bet the little fucker has already sold my idea. I'm going to sue and sue and sue . . . As for that ingenue . . . she's not going to last. I give her ten days before she's on the plane back to her mommy . . . but oh! She's good enough to eat . . . come to my arms, you innocent, you Jamesian heroine . . . Inside ten days—I'll make a bet with you—I'll have laid you, and got my story back from that little queen. Not story. Idea for a treatment. But a germ that could infect the whole world. *(She's still munching pills.)* I feel strange. These are garlic aren't they? No smell . . . *(Falls back on the couch.)* It's a trap. Roger knew I was listening. He's poisoned me. He's got it. The secret. And now he's going to pretend it's his. No kidding! I really am dying! I can see the stern sergeant! He's looking really mean! And now—the blackness! Mother—goodnight! What have I done? What have I done?

Music swells and MERCEDES *falls back clenching her eyes shut, extending her arms to form a cross.*
Music is Handel's 'Behold the Lamb of God'
We hear it rich and sweet. The lighting begins to change and become stronger cue by the building of the choruses into the oratorio.
It fades down enough to allow MERCEDES *to speak.*

MERCEDES *(as if entranced still with her eyes closed).*   I call before
   the eyes two figures, in chains, a man and a woman, yes . . .
   that's right, take the manacles off her so that she can stand upright . . .
   You can burn the man . . . flay him first though . . . the woman . . .
   you can leave her with me . . . Giver her a good . . . education . . .
   (pause) Let me alone now, let me . . . sleep . . . All through the
   nights they put the jets over here, no-one lives, office area, don't let
   me sleep, take her away now, let me sleep . . .

Music fades.
Huge amounts of light coming in from the blind, trapped in the baldes.
Light on set reverts to dim as if it were day with the blinds drawn.
MERCEDES *suddenly bounds springily across the room to pick up*
the phone on the desk, which has not rung.

MERCEDES *(to phone).*   How did I know? Precognition. Of course we
   can talk. Are you alone? I'm alone, of course the sun's trying to come
   in. No, it means I'm in deep trouble. Bye for now. *(Puts down the*
   phone. Talks to the sun behind the blind, from behind the back of
   of her hand.) D'you want to come in now? *(pause)* OK, please
   yourself . . . *(Dialling on the phone, cradling the receiver on her*
   neck.) Deep trouble . . . *(pause)* Dr Robert? Hi. I know I'm late for
   our psychoanalysis by phone, because I've just had a reproachful
   dream about you. No, I can't tell you the details, it wasn't that
   important. Look buddy you get paid by me and I get to tell you the
   important dreams out of the portfolio of the night, and I can tell
   you for free—ha ha—that my dream about being late for you scores
   a big round zero as far as I'm concerned. What d'you mean I've only
   got five minutes? I'm **that** late? I paid for an hour. OK so you got
   to get some sleep in New York. Go to sleep later. OK so I've hurt
   you, sorry. Yes you're right, it was an important dream. It must have
   lasted around fifty five minutes. That's right, this dream is really
   coming between us in a big way. Doctor Robert, is it a symptom of
   my illness that the only thing wrong with our relationship is a guilt
   dream which went on for so long that it's effects carried over into
   real life and here I am saying to you I'm sorry I dreampt about you?
   I mean, surely you have a dream, right, because of the things that
   happen in the world, and not vice versa. And another thing, are
   my biorhythms too much for you? You don't know what biorhythms are? Neither do I, but here I am on this bright sunny
   morning on the West Coast and you're sitting in some over-stuffed
   armchair in New York, in the dark . . . I bet your room's over
   furnished. Did you ever see the photo of Freud's room, taken the
   day before he got chased out of Vienna? Talk about over furnished.
   It looked like a Turkish whore's dressing room. You could barely
   get to the couch. He had to sit at the head of it because there was
   nowhere else to sit down . . . I saw it in a magazine. Does it matter
   that I'm not lying on the couch? You though I was? OK, OK, we'll

61

start again. *(Flips the phone over to intercom and goes to lie on the couch. Instead she gets a glass of water.)* Say if you can't hear me. *(Pacing about, drinking. Inspects another garlic pills, discards it.)* No, I'm fine in myself. I'm holding down a good job—in fact I was almost promoted. I guess that doesn't mean much to you, being a shrink, shrinks are shrinks, aren't they, you don't ever get . . . promoted. A steady job in the film industry, but I can't communicate with people, if my mother was here in the room I couldn't communicate with her. Are you taking any of this in. Doctor Robert, Doctor Robert are you there? Are you awake?*(Screams into intercom.* Doctor Robert?

ROBERT's *voice from miles away with long distance enhanced echo. Mittel european accent.*

ROBERT. Yes . . . ?

MERCEDES. Can't you put your back into your side of the conversation. It's like talking into a vacuum! *(Pause).*

ROBERT. Have you told your mother you're a lesbian?

MERCEDES. Yes. She said she'd rather have given birth to a mass murderer.

ROBERT. How does she feel toward mass murderers?

MERCEDES. Less than forgiving.

ROBERT. How about your hysterectomy?

MERCEDES. I haven't had one yet. But I will. And then I'll tell her.

ROBERT. How old are you?

MERCEDES. I just flunked out of medical school.

ROBERT. Twenty-one? Last week you were thirty-five, and you'd already had the operation.

MERCEDES. I've regressed.

ROBERT. We were making progress.

MERCEDES. The doctors in this country will tell you anything so that they can get their hands up you for a hundred bucks a minute. And I was going to be a surgeon! I got brilliant marks for theory but the bastards blackballed me because they said I had dirty hair and teeth and fingernails and no bedside manner—do you think they'd have dared if I were a man? I want to be a **woman** doctor. And treat people because I love them. Blow the whole shitty infrastructure of capitalism apart with free abortion on demand—health is the right of every woman. And they don't get it. And because they don't get it, it's taken as proof that we need a capitalist medical system.

ROBERT. It's been good to talk to you, Mercedes.

MERCEDES. You can't—don't **leave** me.

ROBERT. My next patient has tied himself to the oil pipeline in Alaska and is threatening to blow himself up. I've got to go. Talk to you tomorrow. 'Bye for now.

MERCEDES. You hundred dollar an hour whore! *(Pause)* He's not a cure for a disease, he's a symptom. He just hung up on me. After

asking how old I am he goes and exhibits totally childish
behaviour. How old am I? How many layers does an onion have?
I'm as old now as I was when I first got afraid of aeroplanes—

*Aeroplane noise advancing surreally, building very quickly into a
terrific shriek. The light from behind the blind dims as if a gigantic
body were crossing the sun.*
MERCEDES *cowers in the middle, her hands over her head. The
noise recedes, and the place goes back to normal.*

MERCEDES. The rest is silence. I was not Prince Hamlet, nor was
ever meant to be . . . The rest is silence. Good. *(fierce)* Thank you,
William Shakespeare . . . For rattling my bones . . . I left yours
alone. Will Shakespeare. Shake—Spear. Will. Shakespear. Phallus
waves itself in the air. Willy? Shakes is ambiguous. Shakespeare: a
good lay, a bad soldier, kissed and girls and boys and then went
home? My ducats, my daughter—a jewel in the crown of three
hundred years of polished antisemitism, and we don't have to
look as far back as Marlowe. 'The jew is underneath the lot.'
'The red eyed scavengers are creeping from Kentish Town and
Golders Green.' If I had you here, Tom Eliot, I'd give your bones
a good kicking. Karl Marx is allowed to be antisemitic, not you.
What I like is the way the gold stuff jumps right into your hand.
Holds out hand) Nothing there yet. Here we are, a mere thirty
floors up from the San Andreas fault, there must be tons of that
symbol of alchemical perfection stuck down there in the earth . . .
come on mother . . . Nothing again nothing? The hairs are standing
up on the back on my neck. That is a code. Message from preh-
history. Yes! The earth is moving. *(Dull brief rumble)* I don't
mind **that**. It's the aeroplanes. I was—in Ankara—nine o'clock in
the morning. Don't ask me what I was doing. Two passenger planes
collided in the clear blue sky over the city. One of them split right
open and **people** . . . raining down like screaming dolls smashing
into the streets, smashing through roofs and houses. Some of them
blazing like stuntmen as they fell—Thank God blind before they
sliced into the telegraph wires that ran between the acacias in the
street and wham into a cloud of dust and jam, and the chickens
clucking and great spits of the plane came down in the market and
round about the suburbs, burning, and there was no more morphine
in the hospital, and the smell which hung over the bruised and half
burnt city, so now I won't travel by aeroplane. I may not be the
right sex—yet—for holistic Tellurian sacrifice, but I can do you a
mean miracle, sidestepping the whole sluggish business of thesis
antithesis leading to synthesis. OK so where's the money? *(Pause)*
I'm going to need it to sue this company. *(A heavy Marlovian
interpretation)* 'Good morning to the day and next, my gold.'
Yeah. But if Elijah could be winched to safety in full view of the
Assyrians in 1500 BC by something which is quite obviously

an Israeli army helicopter, then surely, I can get enough bread together to maintain control over my own artistic ideas. Look at it this way. Jesus Christ was mainly the result of a cheesey long running Jewish rumour—so the chances as fifty fifty that they would even have noticed if he had been a woman. Or maybe close friends did and that's why they switched bodies on the cross . . . There's no evidence either way after all this time. Not much point in coming up with a fragment of the True Fallopian tube . . . Of course, there's always the female pope in the Tarot, maybe her time has come . . . *(She goes over to where the fridge stood.)* If I weren't so hungry I could work it out . . . What's this? *(Picks up an apple.)* A beautiful, dusty little old apple . . . *(Polishes it on her dress.)* Don't look so sad, little one, I'm going to make you so pretty . . . *(Eats it and looks at watch.)* This is going to have to be breakfast, dinner, lunch and breakfast. This is also going to have to be *faute de mieux* the alchemical apple of knowledge—*(Expands her head dramatically with her hands.)*—Poing!! However it is also full of mucilage and vitamins and bran and will produce an only partly symbolic turd. *(Finishes apple.)* Christ was definitely constipated. A childhood forced diet of Egyptian figs—'Eat up go on. Another fig. Just one more, to please your Mommy'. He gets to hate figs. And then in later life JC's walking down the road with his friends, and to their complete astonishment Poum! He blasts a fig tree. She blasts a fig tree. It is a woman. One for you, mother. Women are going to be big next year. Bigger than sharks. Bigger than 'Jaws'. *(Phone rings* MERCEDES *answers it. Deadpan.)* Sorry? Am I going to take my clothes off for the condominium opposite like I usually do at this time of night? Well, I wasn't planning it. Well, no, I wasn't planning it. Well, no, I wasn't aware I made a habit of it. I bought you all binoculars? The whole block? This is not my bedroom, this is a movie producer's office. We're making The Life of Jessica Christ. It's set in modern times. Everything always is, I know. The refurbished deity arrives in a helicopter. The pidgin English for helicopter is 'Mixmaster him Jesus Christ'. Herod's picked it up on his radar in the outer galaxy. He's attempting to screw the timing of the event by launching his own Star of Bethlehem before JC arrives, but they know about that and their trump card is she comes into the world aged 21 and throws paraquat all over the figtree. The Wedding feast at Cana. Sounds like Winegate. The feeding of the 5000, it's a credit card hoax. Walking on water—windsurfing. Healing the sick and raising the dead . . . the great American medical system, of course. Jessica teams up with Martha to form a woman's group in Jerusalem, and we get a lot of publicity about the filming of the crucification with people saying it's tasteless sado-masochistic kitsch. Yes. That's the screenplay, roughly. I think you've got the wrong floor for the stripper. Good luck. *(Phone down.)* I haven't phoned my mother. To tell her . . . *(Dialling)* Oh my god . . .

Mother? Have I woken you? Good. *(aside)* This corocodile has been
slowed down with seconal. You have just fifteen seconds before it
wakes up and begins to bite. Mother I just wanted to tell you I'm a—
mass murderer. No, sorry, I mean I.ve failed my medical exams. I
know I got straight A's but they failed me on appearance. They said
no-one could believe I could cure people. Yes, I'm disappointed too,
being a doctor you could get to meet a lot of nice . . . doctors. That's
just what I though. It's a conspiracy. Against all women. If you've
noticed it mother, then why are you going through the roof at me.
How do you think I feel? I was the one who failed, not you. I know
you haven't made that singular differentiation yet, but it'll come.
No, I'm not going to kill myself. The truth is, it's no great loss that
I won't get to meet all those men, by pressing my stethoscope
against their hairy chests. Sure I did that in training. No, nothing
below the waist. How are your haemorroids? *(pause)* Mother? You
know I told you I was a mass murderer. Well I'm not. Something
else. D'you remember dad saying that homosexuality stood in the
same relation to heterosexuality as capitalism to communism—it
was a phase you went through. Well I'm a capitalist. Did you hear
that mother? Well why are you still talking about your ass? Look
I'll start again. It's very simple. I've got something very important
to tell you. No it can't be as important as what you've got to say.
OK you win. *(Pause)* Say that again. My father's **dead**? And
you didn't tell me because you thought it might affect the grades
of my exams. They were a month ago. I was failed because I
didn't look like Dr Kildare—I can't believe it. Why did you do
this to me? *(Screams)* I have a brilliant mind unaffected by
disaster and you will use any pretext to come between me and
my father! Who killed him? I want to know! He was too young,
some drunken anaesthetist went to a piss—no-one dies that young.
Where is he? **Burned**? I could have done an autopsy. And you
stopped me coming to the cremation—you pig. I bet you killed
him. *(Phone down. Bursts into tears. Dials a number desperately.)*
Doctor Robert—can youhear me? I'm very upset *(Blubbing)*
A close friend of mine has died—my father—Doctor?

VOICE FROM THE INTERCOM.   This is an answering service. Dr
Robert is not available for consultation, as he is on a Morpheus
Fellowship. Our branch office in Hawaii is now open for the
business of the day—

MERCEDES *(puts the phone down on the message. Recovered, goes
to window, looks out sidelong).*   Well . . . Well? If I poured gas
over myself, lit it, jumped smashed through the plate glass and
fell, with my luck I'd land in the swimming pool. Nowhere to turn.
(She hoists up the blind. Outside it is night. Thinking about jumping)
Thesis—antithesis—synthesis.
Chaos—farce, and then the leap into the abyss.

Burning, burning . . .

A rumble of thunder.
The stage darkens.
Music: The 'Mars' Section from Holst's 'Planets'
Outside in the dark, as the music builds, we see the shadowy
silhouette of a man in a bowler hat and overcoat with an umbrella,
huge against the sky.
Wind noises.
The figure stoops with one hand on the hat. The umbrella dives this way
and that and finally flies away.

MERCEDES.   Dad? Is that you? *(Thunder. The wind dies away. The*
   figure retrieves the umbrella and folds it away.) How did you die?
FATHER's VOICE *(resonant, deep, ghostly).*   Mercedes, is that you?
MERCEDES.   Yeah, are you coming in?
FATHER.   No, I can't, I've only got a minute.
MERCEDES.   They stopped me coming to the funeral!
FATHER.   Believe me, you didn't miss much.
MERCEDES.   They won't let me be a doctor.
FATHER.   I died under the doctor. The anaesthetist went for a
   pisssss *(the sibilant gets picked up in the wind rising.)*
MERCEDES.   I got straight A's but they said I smelled!
FATHER.   And that was that. But I've changed my opinion about
   doctors. Who wants that kind of responsibility? Not that they look
   after you here—
MERCEDES.   It looks pretty windy out there!
FATHER.   The food's terrible too. All you ever get to drink is
   sacrificial blood, but *(snide)* you should see what the vegetarian ghosts
   have to eat.
MERCEDES.   What's that?
FATHER.   Asphodels. Nothing grows here much, because of the
   weather, except this little flower shaped like a prick. They're called
asphodels. I had one look and asked to go straight back on a meat diet.
MERCEDES.   What should I do?
FATHER.   Is there any way you could get me some bagels?
MERCEDES.   I'm right out of food food here myself! Listen I failed
   my degree and I found out I'm gay—
FATHER.   And on the tv, they're always showing the same movies—
MERCEDES.   What?
FATHER.   The same movies!
MERCEDES.   What should I do?
FATHER.   Maybe if your mother wrote one of her letters— com-
   plaining—yes that's it—tell her to write to them—
MERCEDES.   What am I going to **do** with my life?
FATHER.   Whatever you do—it's a good thing you never were a
   surgeon, you never washed your hands. Maybe you marry some—
(A siren starts up) That's the lunch bell. I'm off. Wish me luck. Get

66

your mother to write a letter—

The siren swells, the wind blows, the wraith like shadow melts and vanishes.
MERCEDES *goes to the phone.*

MERCEDES Mother? I've just seen his ghost. He said it would be OK
for me to go into the movie business. He said there are openings—
they're crying out for new stuff. I dunno where. Start at the
bottom and work up. Of course I know my father's dead. My
feelings? I can't rise to the moment like you, I didn't give him the
heart attack . . . Look if you spend all his life insurance on getting
me some Mexican medical qualification, I shall have to support you
all the rest of your miserable life. What do you mean? You'll live
for years. I've got to split. Mother I'm a . . . Mother I'm going to
have to write to you. *(Puts phone down and starts to compose a
letter at the desk.)* She's going to drop dead when she reads this.
Assassination by post . . . They'll never catch me! *(Scrumples the
letter up and throws it in the bin. Lets the blind down.)* I'm not
having those peepers over my shoulder at a moment like this.
Mother . . . Who am I **talking** to when I write a letter to my
mother? Who is my mother? *(Genuine bewilderment.)* Isn't
everything a letter to someone or other, a sigil, a sign? Wordsworth
even wrote to god: 'Dear God, the very houses seem asleep . . . '
No. Uneasy. Deep trouble. Flunked the confrontation with mother,
flunked self slaughter, and flunked the course at Wittenberg
University. That is, Wittenberg, North Dakota. *(Sounds of a
helicopter approaching.* MERCEDES *goes to the blind to look out.)*
Hey what's going on out there? There's a helicopter and below it
these bright lights. It's either carrying a car with it's lights on or
I'm the first guy to see something fucking a flying saucer—*(Noise
getting louder)* He's coming too close—Oh my god—he's hit the side
of the condominium—he's losing height—he's lost a blade—he's
coming in here! *(Darkness and terrific crashing sounds* MERCEDES
dives under desk.) I'm getting out of here!

*The lights show wreathing smoke and a scene of destruction. Through
the venetian blind pokes the front half of a Cadillac. It's at a thirty
degree angle, the nose pointing up.*
Outside a distant explosion and a flash as the helicopter explodes.
MERCEDES *walks back into the smoke and dust.*
ROGER UNGLESS *is sprawled over the bonnet of the car. He wears
torn black leather. He is covered in blood, unrecognisable.*
*The car makes a noise and starts to tip. It's obviously balanced, about
to fall.* ROGER'S *foot is wrapped around a steel hawser.*
A distant moaning.
Blood pours on to the floor from ROGER *in a small steady stream,
venous and arterial.*

MERCEDES *puts the wastepaper basket underneath him to catch the drips. He's trapped. There's not much else she can do. She looks at him upside down.*
Click of cooling metal. Car rocks to and fro. Pause. IRENE *climbs out of the car. Tight leather jacket, green make-up on face and arms, sci-fi gun. Clear polythene leggings, cross gartering and sandals.*

IRENE. Where's the pool?

MERCEDES. Thirty floors down.

IRENE. We were meant to land in the pool. And then escape.

MERCEDES. Can I have one of your leggings for a tourniquet?

IRENE. Sure. Can't he come off there?

MERECEDES. The car's about to fall backwards out of the window.

IRENE. The pilot said there wasn't enough room for us in between the buildings, but the director said . . . *(*MERCEDES *takes legging and ties it around* ROGER'S *upper thigh.)* You a doctor?

MERCEDES. Failed.

ROGER. Don't touch me. Just leave me alone. I'll be alright. *(Pulls out a gun, still upside down.)* Both of you, put your hands in the air. *(*IRENE *and* MERCEDES *do so.)*

IRENE. But she was trying to help your bleeding . . .

ROGER. It won't do you any good. Lie down on the floor. Facing away. That's right. *(They do so, facing downstage.)* You there lie down!

IRENE. We are.

ROGER. Lie down I say lie down lie down lie down lie down!

He hauls himself up to almost the right way round and fires at an imaginary person. Then he collapses and drops the gun.
He's dead.
MERCEDES *and* IRENE *get up shakily.*

MERCEDES *(indicating* ROGER). Who . . . ?

IRENE. I dunno. I came in at the last moment as the stuntman's double.

MERCEDES. Oh, a movie.

IRENE. Yeah, he said he'd get killed. *(Looks around the room.)* We really are way off target.

MERCEDES. The pilot lost a blade.

IRENE. He had to get drunk to do it.

MERCEDES *(indicating* ROGER). Was he a friend?

IRENE. No, I said, I never seen him before.

MERCEDES. What kind of movie was it?

IRENE. I don't know.

MERCEDES. Any stars? *(*IRENE *shrugs)* Who was the producer?

IRENE. Search me . . .

She lies on the couch and takes a half bottle of Southern Comfort out of her pocket. Takes a swig and passes it to MERCEDES. *Takes it back before she can drink any.*

MERCEDES.   How are we going to get out of here?

IRENE.   Elevator?

MERCEDES.   We might, but the helicopter's knocked them off the side of the building.

IRENE.   I've had nothing but rotten luck all day. Still, this is comfortable.

MERCEDES.   It's a casting couch.

IRENE.   No kidding.

MERCEDES.   The old man used to make movies but then he died. I took over from him.

IRENE *(cool).*   Wow-wee.

MERCEDES.   Something the matter?

IRENE.   I'm starting to be in shock, that's all.

MERCEDES.   What's your name?

IRENE.   Irene.

MERCEDES.   My mother was called Irene. It means 'Peace'.

IRENE.   Does it really now. That's nice. What's your name?

MERCEDES.   Mercedes. *(IRENE laughs.)* Something wrong?

IRENE.   Sounds like a smart sedan . . .

MERCEDES.   It's Spanish for Mary of Mercies.

IRENE *(giggling).*   . . . Cruising round the block eyeing the girls. I can just see you. Sorry I didn't mean to offend you.

MERCEDES.   I've lived with the problem for some time.

IRENE.   And now you're mad at me.

MERCEDES.   You should have seen me with my mother.

IRENE.   Was she in here?

MERCEDES.   No, she's . . . dead.

IRENE.   Dead. *(MERCEDES feeling the pulse of ROGER.)* I feel completely **gone**. Hey, doctor, are you going to feel my pulse? *(MERCEDES does so. Puts the arm down.)* Well?

MERCEDES *(offhand).*   It's nothing to write home about.

IRENE.   Here, look, it's just because I'm **cold**. Give us a hug. *(MERCEDES holding off. IRENE holding out her hands.)* What's the matter?

MERCEDES.   I . . . fear you. Slightly. As being not entirely human. But perhaps . . . something . . . to do with me.

IRENE.   This is just green paint. It comes off.

MERCEDES *(whispers).*   My mind's not right. Are you not the same Irene that . . .

IRENE.   I want company here on this settee.

MERCEDES *(inches her way over).*   I know this is dangerous.

IRENE.   What is? I don't know what you're **talking** about.

MERCEDES.   I've got to call my mother first.

IRENE.   Go ahead. What are you going to tell her?

MERCEDES.   I'm going to tell her I met this really nice girl who fell out of a helicopter.

IRENE. Cool.

MERCEDES. And we have something in common . . .

IRENE. Telepathy! Hey but I thought you said your mother
was dead.

MERCEDES. She's dead to the civilised world. She only speaks
pidgin English.

IRENE. Will she know what a helicopter is then?

MERCEDES. Oh yes, she's from a cargo cult tribe. *(Phones
at the desk)* Mother? It's me. Er Mixmaster him belong Jesus
Christ all gone for bush belong ban fuckup, Mercedes belong
boss chick wantie muchee jig jig, toujours toujours unmade bed.
(Pause. Phone down. About to take off tights.) She say's it's
fine.

IRENE. Would you do something for me first. Would you get me
an apple out of the car. They're in the glove compartment.

MERCEDES *(goes to the car and gets an apple).* Do you have any
more of these?

IRENE *(faint).* No . . . don't eat it . . . please . . . *(arms outstretched
piticully.)*

MERCEDES. But I'm **hungry**.

IRENE. If you eat it, I'll fade away . . .

MERCEDES. Just one bite? *(IRENE shakes her head.)* Please.
(Statis.) I'm going to take one bite and then give all the rest to
you. I haven't eaten for days.

MERCEDES *takes a bite. We hear a hugely exaggerated scrunch and
chomping on the sound system synchronously.*
The lights begin to change to blue and green.
IRENE faints in this looking like The Death of Chatterton'

IRENE I told you . . . *(Faints.)*

MERCEDES *(goes to her and tries to pull her up and revive her).* Irene!
Don't be so cold to me, don't be cold . . . *(She fails to revive* IRENE.
Then rapidly grows annoyed.) Oh, fuck it. Why do I always fall for
the wrong kind of temptation? *(Defiantly)* Not my fault! I was under
orders from my stomach. Hunger done bite-Um . . .

Blackout.
*A dimly lit stage. The couch and desk have been pushed back and
midstage is a gigantic fridge. It is the same fridge as at the beginning
of the play but now it is huge, an imposing icon.*
*Round the base is a huge thick rope, which ties two firework
rockets to the fridge, one each side. These are without their sticks,
thick tubes with gaily painted scenes of skies alight with roman
candles etc. and a proprietary name on the side.*
*Steam hisses from a vent underneath the fridge and half way
up the side like an Apollo launch.*
Music.

Opening chords as we build the lighting on this wonderful object.
ROGER UNGLESS *is fussing round the base of the monument.*
He has a white lab coat on and a clip-board. He has a stick-on
droopy moustache. He looks a bit like Albert Einstein. His voice
is the voice he uses for Mercedes' father.
He is standing by a teaspoon seven-foot long with some yellowish
mayonnaise on it, in a lump.
He puts a small step-ladder at the side of the edifice and climbs up
it as the music fades. He searches for MERCEDES *in the dark*
of the auditorium.

ROGER.   Hey! You! Come out of there!

He pulls MERCEDES *on to the stage. She is clutching a piece of*
salami five-foot in diameter, rolled up, and a piece of white stuff,
not necessarily immediately identifiable.
She faces ROGER, *her 'FATHER'. She's dressed a bit like a little*
girl, but no attempt should be made to Mabel Lucy Atwellise her.

ROGER.   What's this? What's this? *(He throws the white chunk*
    behind the fridge.)
MERCEDES *(childish, unmoved).*   It's an egg I was eating.
ROGER.   And this! And this! *(Wrenches the salami off her and*
    throws it behind as well.)
MERCEDES.   Salami. I was eating that too.
ROGER *(pointing at the spoon).*   And this! And this!
MERCEDES *(goes and tries it, takes a little lick off her finger).*
    Hellman's Mayonnaise.
ROGER.   You know what? You're going to be the death of me!
MERCEDES.   What d'you mean Dad?
ROGER.   No better—worse! You're going to get us all killed!
MERCEDES.   I just took a snack out of the refrigerators.
ROGER *(points to rockets).*   What's this?
MERCEDES.   It's a refrigerator.
ROGER.   No it's not. I've changed it. I've changed it into a rocket.
MERCEDES *(blithely).*   OK . . .
ROGER.   But you've eaten half the fuel!
MERCEDES.   I only had a tiny bite.
ROGER.   I got a launching in about ten minutes. Test launching
    for King Herod. He's very worried. In fact he's in deep trouble.
    See, there's a cast iron prophecy, that sometime in the next
    year, a guy's going to be born to be king of the Jews. Going to
    be born in Bethlehem.
MERCEDES.   So you're going to wipe it off the map with a
    rocket attack? You won't be able to aim that straight.
ROGER.   Let me finish will you? The signal for when he's born
    is a watchamacallit, you know, a whimwam to wind up the
    sun, a comet or something, stuck up there in the sky over
    Bethlehem. So Herod asks me to make a decoy, to send up

first. Then he can move in and arrest the troublemakers. This is the prototype. See, soon as this little baby gets moving the phlogiston in the salami will catch alight in the speed of passage and it will be seen hurtling across the heavens, brighter than any star.

MERCEDES. I guess there'll always be people like you around ready to tackle dubious contracts.

ROGER. It's a straight law and order job.

MERCEDES. Yeah, well suppose the real guy isn't going to be what he's cut out to be by the opposition. Suppose he isn't this all-fired workingclass firebrand? Suppose he's **meek**? And **gentle** like a lamb. How d'you feel then if he got flushed out and clubbed to death because of your invention? Dad—what if he was a **good man**? Huh?

IRENE *comes in.*
Hair greased back, black T-shirt, jeans, fiddling the ground with her foot like James Dean.

ROGER. It doesn't matter even if he was a woman. If he was as good a woman as your poor dead mother it'd still be necessary on account of law and order. Anyhow, it's not going to be a woman. Was Abraham a woman?

IRENE *(James Dean like).* Yeah. Yeah, Abraham was a woman.

ROGER. Get that boy out of here. He's nothing but trouble.

IRENE *slouches over to* MERCEDES *and openly kicks her on the arse.*

MERCEDES. Hey! What was that for?

IRENE' Being fat.

MERCEDES *(grabs* IRENE *and half-nelsons 'him' to his knees.* IRENE'S *face screwed up in pain but with no sound).* Say that again.

IRENE *(whisper).* You're hurting me.

MERCEDES. Say that again.

Stasis. ROGER *goes about fiddling with the fuses of the rockets, laying out more fuse etc.*

ROGER. There are sound biological reasons why women can't be religious or political leaders. For a start, women are weaker. Let your brother go there. You see people like to associate institutions with continuity. Women are not continuous. The whole race of women. Splitting open like water melons to produce another from within. One moment down, the next swollen like balloons. When a woman nurses, her breasts enlarge. When a man governs, does his head enlarge . . . women are self interested. The zeal of the penis is easily extraverted into building programmes, trade and massacres. Women have always recognised this and have

wisely elected men to govern them. Pull yourselves together
you two, here comes Herod. *(MERCEDES abruptly exits.
ROGER turns to IRENE who rubs her shoulder and gets up.)*
I don't know what to do with that sister of yours. If only
she'd get herself a man—Not one of your Greek friends,
either. I say you coming up the stairs with a boy last night.
Why d'you do it? Nasty foreign habit. If you stick with boys
the wind'll change and you'll find you'll be that way for
life. It happened to a friend of mine. *(Trumpets sound off
raucous and loud.)*

IRENE. I prefer boys.

ROGER *(resigned).* Have it your own way then—

Trumpets again.
*A sedan chair inches on. It has four naked black slaves carrying
it: they are cutouts on the ends of the poles. MERCEDES in the
middle surrounded by royal purple, wearing an Abyssinian spade
beard, and crown.*

VOICE. His royal Highness King Herod, King of the Kingdom of
Judea, King of the Jews.

More trumpets.
IRENE watches.
ROGER does a perfunctory abasement and gets up.

ROGER. Your highness we are ready for the trial firing.

MERCEDES Good. *(To IRENE)* You're a pretty boy, what's
your name? *(IRENE just stares.)* Is this going to work?

ROGER. I'd stake my reputation on it.

MERCEDES. Payload looks too large for the thrust. Stake your
life on it?

ROGER. Whatever your Highness pleases. Light the fuse, boy.

MERCEDES. Matches! *(IRENE throws a book of matches on the
floor. ROGER picks them up and lights a fuse leading to the
rocket.)* Funny thing happened to me on the way here. I
discovered **boys**. I thought, I'm thirty-eight and I've never had a
boy.

ROGER. We should stand well back.

MERCEDES. So I had one. **Delicious**.

ROGER. Stand back.

MERCEDES. I stopped the royal procession on the other side of
Golgotha and there was a **boy**, ploughing the stony soil pushing
the plough, no animals. So I said, would you like to get down on
your hands and knees, boy, I asked politely. And he did! Isn't
that marvellous? We did say your life was on this, didn't we?
Good. I'm looking forward to this.

The rockets launch. Authentic NASA rumble. Plenty of smoke

and flare from underneath the fridge. Rolling clouds of smoke.
IRENE still upstage, MERCEDES and ROGER downstage.
The fridge lifts off the ground slowly two or three feet then
settles as slowly back into position. The flaring and rumbling
dies. Smoke billows and rolls everywhere.
Lights slowly change to a central pool.
The smoke clears. We see ROGER, *curled up dead with a sword*
in his gut. On either side, MERCEDES *and* IRENE *facing each*
other, over the corpse. Lights fading fast.

MERCEDES.   Come here, little jew-boy. Show me something I
   don't know. *(Blackout.* MERCEDES' *voice)* Operator. This
   is urgent. I keep ringing my emergency psychiatrist and the
   only people who answer are the Hawaiian Fire Brigade. I must
   have left a cigarette burning in the trash can because the place
   is full of smoke. When I woke up, I rang the janitor, but he gave
   me this line about everything being fireproof. So I figured I'm
   crazy. I ring up my shrink, and who do I get but the Hawaiian
   Fire Brigade. No, there's no fire, just smoke.

Lights. The fridge has gone but the set is still full of smoke. The
blind is down at the back. MERCEDES *in her clothes as at the*
beginning is pacing through the gloom. On the phone at the
couch. Dialling.

MERCEDES.   Mother? How's Dad? I can't tell you what a
   relief that is. I've had the most—enough nightmares to last me
   a lifetime. First I was fired from my job, then I was back at
   college failing my masters and then this car came through the
   window—What? What do you mean who am I? I'm your
   daughter. Well, if I'm not your daughter, who the fuck have
   I been talking to? *(The other end hangs up.)* We'll never know.
   No. My mother's rejected me. She's blocked my memory. She's
   never had me. I'm alone. And it's four o'clock in the . . .
   morning? Evening? *(A polite cough off stage left.)* Who is it?
VOICE.   The janitor.
MERCEDES.   What's your name?

The ROGER UNGLESS *actor comes on as a feeble* JANITOR,
elderly.

ROGER.   I'm the janitor. You Miss Mercedes Mordecai?
MERCEDES.   Right.

ROGER *exists and re-enters immediately with a fire-extinguisher.*
Goes over to the waste paper basket and points the extinguisher
into it.

ROGER.   Seems to have gone out of its own accord. *(Gives her a*
   pad to sign.) I've got a surprise in the elevator for you. If you'd

sign for it . . . *(pushes on the normal version of the fridge.)* This
is a good old refrigerator. My mother always lusted after one
of these, but we were hogtied poor and the last people in the
whole of California to get electricity. We had a dirt farm, right
here beneath your feet. *(Proud)* We had the sickest chickens in the
valley. I used to hire myself out, lighting fires in the orange
groves to keep the trees warm. At the end, Dad sold out and was
this big time gambler, for about three weeks, then he died. And
now there's just me. Can't get reconciled to being so old. Really
I'm just a boy, but here I am, older than god. *(He sits.)*
MERCEDES *(cold).* Planning to stay long?
ROGER. We don't get many calls, not this time of the night.
   What's your line of business?
MERCEDES. Movie about Jesus Christ.
ROGER. Ah, he didn't ever know what it was like to be old.
MERCEDES. Or have kids.
ROGER. He had all the fun with wine, and women, and then after
   a slight brush with the law, he took off into heaven.
MERCEDES. He was killed first.
ROGER. If he was who he claimed to be, he must have known they
   couldn't kill him. He must have known he was immortal.
MERCEDES. I figure he was a woman.
ROGER. Yeah, just like a woman, to faint at the first sight of
   a nail. Reckon you're right.
MERCEDES. Not what I meant.
ROGER. You can try and show women to be as dumb and
   cringing as you like, but you ain't going to alter the basic fact
   about this country. That it's a matriarchy. There are plenty of
   women like you, all fired up to cut the balls of Jesus one way of
   the other, but as he never had the use of them it seems academic.
   And when you get to my age, it's all the same, anyways.
   You said on the phone you were trying to get through to your
   mother, but your lines got crossed. If you've her address, I could
   get my son Tom to drive over there. He's a packer, but he's got
   six kids so he's got to work nights driving a radio taxi. *(Dialling)*
   Martha? This is Tom's pa. Can you hook me up to him? Is he
   anywhere near 4626 Acacia? Get him to go in and tell the woman
   her daughter's been trying to ring her. Name's Mordecai. *(Holds
   the phone in his lap.)* It's a sad business when your folks don't
   answer. A long time since mine been dead. As a matter of fact,
   I never believed in them until they did die, I always thought
   some shiny black Cadillac was going to stop right outside and
   a couple in fur coats would take me away from all that unintell-
   igible poverty. But they never did come through those gates.

Switches the phone to intercom and lays the receiver on the desk.

MERCEDES *looks at him. He folds his hands and head down appears to snooze.*
He wakes as the intercom comes to life. Excited redneck voice.

VOICE. Dad? This is Tom. I've been to the address. It's in the middle of a trailer park, and all the lights were on, and there was this gas-log fire burning in the grate, and a meal for three at the table—heavy silver—but there ain't no-one there. It's like they vanished off the face of the earth.

ROGER. He always was keen on 'Startrek'. *(Nods wisely.)*

MERCEDES. Try the launderette!

ROGER. It's a one way link, he can't hear you.

VOICE. Hey! Dad! I think I can see something moving in the sky—Dad—look out east of the window—

ROGER *gets himself up laboriously and winds up the blind. We see the horizon with a few streaks of pink.*
A bright light, not large, traverses slowly from right to left.

ROGER *(resigned).* It's one of them Ufo's.

VOICE *(uninterested).* It's one of them Ufo's. *(Noise of car engine turning but not firing.)* Goddamit. Fuckers always stall my engine.

ROGER *(hangs up on him).* You'd have thought with that amount of family responsibility he'd larn to control his language. Someone ought to talk to that boy.

MERCEDES. Will he go after it if he can get started?

ROGER. He's got a living to earn, he'd be wasting his time. You see them so often you end up losing interest. Tell you something really interesting that happened to me the other day. Now Tom, he took me up in an airplane. Birthday treat. Five or six of us. And the man sitting next to us died of a heart attack. A mile and a half up in the air. We all talked about it for days. Never did get to the bottom of it. I mean, why die if you're having a good time? About half of us were in favour of pitching him out then and there, for spoiling our fun. *(A sly laugh.* MERCEDES *looks at him strangely' The smoke is clearing.)* Don't you get too close now, I'm going to do a little trick for your amusement. *(Covers his face with duster.)* I'm going to take you back in time.

MERCEDES. Wait a minute, who are you?

ROGER *(whipping off the duster).* I can't tell you that, I've got to go down and cook up my breakfast. Look—dawn with her rosy fingers is at it again over there—

Points out of the window: the sky is reddening.
MERCEDES *turns.*
As she turns we hear a cock crow. Once, twice, then a distant clear panoply of farmyard noises.

MERCEDES *(distracted)*.   It's a farm!

ROGER.   Yes, it's the farm I was raised on before the Great
   War, it was right here, beneath your feet. Don't look down—

MERCEDES.   I can smell jasmine.

ROGER.   That's right. Don't look down—*(The noise continues.)*
   Before the movies was even a barn in a field in Hollywood. No
   smog. No atom bomb. No airplanes. A man could stand . . . on
   his land. . . and say . . . Don't look down—No-one was ever up
   this high, in those days greeting the dawn, hearing the whole
   neighbourhood wake up. All these sound have been completely
   unheard until—before the sun—

He steps into the fridge and shuts the door on himself.
The noise gradually peters away to nothing.

MERCEDES *(whisper)*.   Madness is . . . finally here. No, not
   that way.

Quick fade to blackout.

ACT TWO

As before. MERCEDES *on stage, glowering.*
IRENE *arrives, bright as a button*

IRENE. Hello—I'm looking for Miss Mordecai.

MERCEDES *(without turning).* She's out.

IRENE. When's she coming back?

MERCEDES. About forty years. She had an existential crisis.
Got banana oil between the ideas in her brain so they slid
around too fast for her to catch.

IRENE. Who are you?

MERCEDES. I'm her groupie, know what I mean?

IRENE. I recognise your voice, I talked to you on the phone.

MERCEDES. I never talk on the phone. I'm never here.

IRENE. What about now?

MERCEDES. Now is different. Now I'm trying to find out if
her parents are dead.

IRENE. I couldn't help you.

MERCEDES. Well take a running jump through the window
then. *(Pause)* Everyone else does.

IRENE *(taking off her coat to reveal expensive tweedy clothes,
very English).* I heard you were eccentric.

MERCEDES. Yeah.

IRENE. I've come to work as assistant on the film you're
making.

MERCEDES *(tapping her head).* Can you get in there right away
and clean up the cutting room?

IRENE. You've been shooting already?

MERCEDES. Can't you see?

IRENE. I'm sorry, did I come too early for you?

MERCEDES. No, carry on, please.

IRENE. Sorry?

MERCEDES. You heard of the dark night of the soul?

IRENE. It's just that they taught me how early Americans like
to get up and work, and so I decided not to go to bed.

MERCEDES. With who?

IRENE. Whom?

MERCEDES. Whom?

IRENE. With myself. I'm jetlagged. All my biorhythms say it's evening. In fact, d'you have a drink?

MERCEDES. I don't know.

IRENE *goes to the fridge and opens it. Magically, it is full of glasses of chilled Martinis.*
She takes out the tray and puts them within easy reach of MERCEDES *who eats several olives.*

IRENE *(takes sips from a glass)*. I don't know why, but I'm nervous.

MERCEDES. If I had the energy I would be too. Relax. Lie down. Take your shoes off. Anything you like.

IRENE *lies on the couch taking off her shoes and dropping them in to the wastepaper basket. She attempts to relax and takes her glass of Martini.*

MERCEDES *(over to the fridge, slamming the door)*. You seen that refrigerator before?

IRENE. What kind of a question is that?

MERCEDES. It was a kind of a question! Answer me! *(Pause.)* It was a worried question. Not sure whether it has just arrived, or it's already left, or this is a sneak preview for when it comes, later. *(A bosun's whistle, two notes, rising, faint but clear in the pause.* MERCEDES *wrapped up in herself.)* D'you know how to whistle? You just put your lips together and blow—in the film.

IRENE. Sorry?

MERCEDES. Not you. Men—bankers—in Boston Massachussetts, at night, with women in parked cars, or earlier, in ditches hiding from divebombing airplanes different people but all— poisoned—with fear and loathing, the blood that calls out blood, oppression on me who ain't never done nothing. *(Pause)* I'm coming out of it. Sorry. The race is not to the quick for they have too much blood. *(Pause)* I'm out of it now. *(Pause)*

IRENE' What kind of a fridge is that?

MERCEDES. I must apologise for being so unhospitable. *(Faces* IRENE *smiling)* Your naturalness and good manners so put me at my ease that I thoughtlessly includes you in the boundary. of my morbidity. Will you ever forgive me?

IRENE *(complacent)*. Och aye. Tell me about your parents.

MERCEDES. I'm trying to trace them. My parents don't seem to be anywhere. But then I have an exile's aspect in my chart.

IRENE. You believe in it?

MERCEDES. Uh—huh. I heard my mother was in town. But a

man called up on the radio to say she'd disappeared. *(IRENE nods sagely.)* His father, the janitor, he walked through the wall. *(IRENE smiles.)* You don't seem to worried.

IRENE. No. Well I've just had the most wonderful thing happen to me: I got on this big silver bird and it came down in a different country in a different time. It's what I've dreamed of

MERCEDES *(struck).* Hey, Irene, d'you think we could end it just like that, with her going off and up like a rocket in broad daylight, without a twist or anything?

IRENE. You'd better ask the janitor.

MERCEDES. He was something else!

IRENE. Oh, miracles! Tolstoy said that compared to the teachings of our Lord, that the miracles were like a candle in comparison to the sun.

MERCEDES. Tolstoy? This some guy you were in analysis with?

IRENE. County Leo Tolstoy. The writer.

MERCEDES. Oh! He was a Leo was he. A sun sign. Yeah, right. *(Earnest)* Tell me, did you ever get yourself straightened out? When you were in EST?

IRENE. I wasn't.

MERCEDES. Oh! You weren't either. Like me. *(Proud)* My experience of EST is not having had it. What's your orientation? Sexually.

IRENE. To the sun.

MERCEDES. I'm under the impression that I told my mother I was gay. I have a distinct memory of a phone call.

IRENE. Perhaps your father—

MERCEDES. No! He died when I was at college, before I came out. He couldn't have known, and yet I still feel guilty about that, as if it were his second sight of me which killed him.

IRENE. So what do you think about your mother?

MERCEDES *(wicked glee).* I think, one down and one to go!

IRENE. What's your problem?

MERCEDES. I look out of the window, and I think, I've been here too long. D'you want to come back to my place?

IRENE. To what end?

MERCEDES. To avoid . . . My unpleasant feelings of vertigo.

IRENE. I came for a job. And it wasn't housework.

MERCEDES. Lord knows, I am not good at that. I am not—clean. Not that I don't want to be. Matter comes to me. And sticks.

IRENE. You know you can't take me home.

MERCEDES. I know. I wouldn't be able to support you in the style to which you're being accustomed, because I never go to be producer. I lost my job.

IRENE. Don't you want to talk?

MERCEDES. I don't even want to be kissed goodnight.

IRENE *(suddenly dynamic)*. Wake up! Wake up!

MERCEDES *(grudgingly opens one eye)*. Why?

IRENE. Don't go to sleep on me! Help. Please. The window's
talking to me. It says 'come here' . . . warmly . . .
*(*MERCEDES *is comatose)*. If you can save me Mercedes, I'll
give you anything. Oh! It's so hot in here. I'm so hot . . .
Mercedes. Help me please. I am . . . I want to jump. Hot . . .
(She takes off bracelets and throws them down.) Burning . . .

MERCEDES *(dull)*. No. A giant hand is pressing me down . . . See it
on my chest. Swart . . .

IRENE. Please . . . Not now . . . Why can't you get up and
help me?

MERCEDES. Vertigo. And anyhow, I do know who you are.
You're my **sister**. In the old medieval stories, the devil was
Christ's **brother**, making his way in the world. See? And you're
my sister.

IRENE. Oh no surely not. My clothes are—unless I get in the
cool air outside—

MERCEDES. Stop fidgeting and listen. The devil ran all the
world's trade and got rich. Joseph of Arimathea got ripped
off by him—had to pay double fare for his passage to England.
And he got back just as the devil was taking JC up to the top
of the world trade centre, to show him all the kingdoms of
the world. And Jesus was agreeing to the contract, and
Joseph said—don't touch it, Jesus, the guy's a crook! And
Jesus said, but he's my brother! If I can't trust my family,
he said, who can I trust? And that is why I'm going to come
to the window with you, sister. And look down at some
sportfucking convention or a farm or a flying saucer, or
something else that isn't there. I wouldn't come even if you
brought me my mother's head on a plate, with her own
mayonnaise . . .

IRENE *(to an invisible attraction at the window)*. Not now—
later—my shoes—

*She bundles towards the window unwillingly, tearing at her
jumper. She gasps pitifully and falls through. Sound of smashing
plate glass. As she does so the wastepaper basket where she has
left her shoes ignites with a woomph and a bright crackle.
Then it smokes nastily while burning.*
MERCEDES *is asleep.*
*A musical, ufonic rumble as the lights slowly return to normal.
The computer rattles a single line of print out.*
MERCEDES *wakes, gets up, finds a soda siphon and squirts
it on to the wastepaper basket. Extinguished.*
The computer printout rattles urgently. MERCEDES *goes
to it.*

MERCEDES. What do you mean she's dead? My mother? Where's the funeral? But she didn't want to be cremated. OK, I understand. You even called a cab. Thank you. I'll be right down.

She lowers the blind and exits.
The computer delivers a final message into the pause.
IRENE *enters at a busy chic secretarial bustle, wearing her 'English' clothes. She puts out bottles of Perrier water on the table. She takes them from a string bag.*
ROGER *enters. He has a natty suit, as at the beginning. He looks like an accountant, or the owner of a successful dry-cleaning shop.*

ROGER *(authoritative)*. Hey, stop that. What are you doing? What's that?

IRENE. It's a fridge. I went down and got these down the street.

ROGER *(feeling a bottle)*. They've got to be cold. That's why we have it here. *(Goes to the fridge. It is full of bottles of Perrier water. He tries to move one out.)* Jesus fucking Christ! They're frozen in solid! What have you done to it girl? Irene? Answer me. Was it you who did this?

IRENE *(busy)*. You said to make sure they were really cold.

ROGER. There are limits!

IRENE *(looking at the printout on the desk)*. Is that the revised budget?

ROGER. This is just projected sales from spinoffs. Records and T shirts.

IRENE *(looking)*. Not a lot.

ROGER. My chicken, you do your job and I'll do mine.

IRENE. All I have to do I've done. Data release is slow.

ROGER. I'm blocking it.

IRENE. You can't forever.

ROGER. You know why the whole financial structure of this film is threatened? Unless we make it a totally subliminal sell, below the threshold of public accountability, unless in fact we get people coming to see the movie in their **sleep**, we're going to be outflanked by the women's movement. That's what this sales graph says to me. It says we're going to get fucked by the women's movement. It's smarter than you. You feed in a number of models: Hegelian, Platonic, even Aristotle's model of the physical world. And they all say the same thing. Women are going to be really big this decade.

IRENE. Who's going to make the tea?

ROGER. Look you left England because you didn't want to be a dolly secretary, and you've made it right?

IRENE. I'm still in hock.

ROGER. Precisely, you are benefitting from the effects of the credit structure. You are freed from the drudgery of paperwork by a databank information system. All you've got to do is de-ice the fridge and zap it to them with that cute English accent. I

82

know everybody ends up having mixed feelings about standing round looking pretty, but it gets you much further than letting your feelings show. *(Pause).* Is there blood on my face?

He gets out a little mirror from his case and starts to trim his moustache.
Noise of approaching plane. It passes, loud.
ROGER *looks up briefly. Back to his wet droopy moustache.*

ROGER.   Hear that? *(Pause)* She's going to cut my throat when she comes in, it's no better than it was. I had six inches of fibre wadding in the ceiling, and **three** layers of glass put in over the weekend. She's going to cut my fucking throat . . . Has she topped you yet?

IRENE.   Sorry?

ROGER.   Has she fucked you yet?

IRENE.   I wish you wouldn't swear. *(She lights a cigarette nervously.)*

ROGER.   No! No! No! *(Leaps over and snatches the cigarette away.)*

IRENE.   I can't smoke?

ROGER.   No. There's around three million dollars worth of information circuitry here. The air is filtered through a cleaner and an antistatic humidifier. If you smoke, you lay this film of effective semiconductor hydrocarbons over the electrics, and fuck it completely. *(He shreds the extinguished cigarette.)* The machine goes fucking barmy. It's so delicate that we've even had to have reinforced glass windows, so they don't crack and let the smog in. So, no, you can't smoke.

IRENE.   Roger, you've taught me something over the last few days since I've been working with you.

ROGER.   Good! What is it?

IRENE.   To the extent that I have learnt from them I'm grateful for the confidences you have offered, about your life, and I'm glad if what you say is true, that is that you have come to this country and found happiness. I don't know what happiness is for you, but it's clear to me that the long struggle for self realisation which so many people in sexual minorities undergo, you have not undergone. Where I am prepared to offer all my sympathies I find in you exactly the same carapace of reflex greed and chauvanism that is meant to be the hallmark of the unconscious and oppressive straight world. In fact when you should be good— better than other people who haven't had to go through what you have—you are rotten. And where you are ignorant, which is just about all over, you should be wise. You have learnt nothing. There is practically no hope for you, even if you spent eternity with your head up your own arse. You are a discredit to the whole of the human race. You have made come true all the cliches, that fall out of people's mouths. You've gathered them together ruthlessly to be your persona. Roger, you are a mincing, ruthlessly ambitious little queen.

Pause.
Enter MERCEDES.
She has a huge floral hat on and a black coat. She throws the hat on the desk. Wearing tennis shoes underneath.
IRENE *helps her off with her coat.*

ROGER *(bright).* Hi there!
MERCEDES *(calm).* Out of my seat, punk. *(*ROGER *doesn't move.)*
ROGER. How was the funeral?
IRENE *(to* ROGER*).* Roger, you are off beam as the jews who wanted to join the National Socialists in 1930. Goering had a joke about them. They could march, with the Nazis but under their own separate banner, which would read, 'We are our own misfortune'.

Pause.
MERCEDES *goes to* ROGER *and lifts him out of the seat by his ear, and then kicks him on the behind.*
ROGER *huffy but in control of himself.*

ROGER. I told her she couldn't smoke.
MERCEDES. Dear Roger. Always a little short on charm. *(She flips Perrier water from the tips of her fingers over* IRENE, ROGER, *and the desk.)* Peace . . . Peace . . .
ROGER. I think if anything water's even worse for it.
MERCEDES. Roger, I brought a plant up in the elevator. Will you get it.
ROGER. Irene.
MERCEDES. Irene's allergic to this particular plant. I want you to get it. *(*ROGER *exits.* MERCEDES *gets out a tiny upright amphora from her bag. Puts it on the table.)*
IRENE. The computer says the film's not an attractive idea financially.
MERCEDES. Yes . . . well, that's probably because of an over emphasis in the model of the Bible Belt penumbra. This technology is only as good as the information you feed into it. We end up making the movie We just happen to be using a couple of sockfulls of sand, and a few electrons to help us. There are various parameters this baby has no way of charting: instance the slow but progressive liberation of women from the mythology of menstrual blood. This thing knows no more than Roger about that, not because it's not a woman, but because we have no suitable models for mythic parameters. *(Pause)* The calculation of mythic parameters used to be called astrology. And there's nothing in popular astrology about the planets determining sexual orientation. Though I did read once that if you wanted a boy, you should fuck pointing at the sun. Or was it the moon?
IRENE *(evading* MERCEDES' *invitation).* That's a nasty little vase.
MERCEDES. The vase? Oh, that's not just a vase, that's my mother.

Or rather the microchip version of my mother. She gave her body to Science, but they ran out of interest when they got to her head, so we cremated it.

IRENE.   What are you going to do with it?

MERCEDES.   Does that bald little creep still bring his macrobiotic lunchbox in, you know, the things he eats with organic hair restorer? Bring it over here.

IRENE *gets a plastic pot from* ROGER'S *case.*

MERCEDES *rapidly sprinkles some dust from the urn into the pot, stirs it in, tastes it, and replaces the lid.*

ROGER *comes back in the room with a pained expression.*

He's carrying a pot plant.

He's distressed.

MERCEDES.   What's the matter, Roger, did someone forget to squeeze your buns?

ROGER.   No. *(Pause)* I don't know what the fuck I'm doing with this plant. *(Drops it.)*

MERCEDES.   What's that on your vest?

ROGER *(looks down).*   Blood.

MERCEDES.   Never mind. Eat first. We'll talk later.

ROGER *(eats a spoonful of his lunch).*   I've been shot.

MERCEDES.   Where?

ROGER.   Just below the sternum. It's bad. I think I'm going to need–

MERCEDES *(snatches up the phone).*   Medicare? I have one very sick accountant. Symptoms? He's been gunned down by the Mafia, and he won't eat his lunch. *(Phone down.)*

IRENE.   He doesn't look well.

MERCEDES.   No! Sick. Very sick. He's not in any shape to tackle my mother.

IRENE.   What a collishangie!

MERCEDES.   I love you Irene. *(Pause)* What do you say?

IRENE.   Well like the enchanted princess in the fairy tale, there's not much I can say to the prince, except, 'I wish you well'.

MERCEDES.   I think we're very much in tune. Don't you?

IRENE.   I need to talk to my mother first.

MERCEDES.   Checkmate! *(A plane starts to go overhead noisily.* MERCEDES *furious at the noise.)* I had this place soundproofed! Shut up will you!

The noise grows deafening. The sky darkens.

IRENE *cowers with her fingers in her ears.*

MERCEDES *(looking for something to express her anger, seizes the plastic pot containing* ROGER'S *lunch and hurls it at the wall).* What a mother . . . *(It bursts and splodges.* IRENE *goes to clean up the mess.)* No, no, leave it, it's probably the best place for her up against the wall. (*IRENE continues.* MERCEDES *sits.* Think about what I said to you huh? *(Pause)* I'm going to sleep now, for . . .

five minutes. I have to be relaxed for this script conference. Get
Roger to launder the dirty money, if he doesn't he's dead. And sound
proof. Tell him . . . the pilots. Young men, sometimes only yards over
head, with the sickness in their blood of too much time . . . reach for
the joystick. It's not there. Sleepwalkers, the present a shadow. Absen
captains of ships of the air . . . over Ankara at nine o'clock one sunny
morning—I shot the Albatross. The control said fog, they lied, I saw
flaming bodies, falling from the high wire of the air . . .

She's asleep.
IRENE *wakes* ROGER *in the fading light. No trace of their earlier dis-*
agreement. They are slipping out of character into function. IRENE
collects the plant and her coat. ROGER *collects his briefcase. They*
tiptoe out.
A bridge passage. Sound and lights of a stream train moving out of a
station mix to sound of control tower talking down a plane.
During this, the telephone rings. MERCEDES *wakes and goes sleepily to*
the desk phone where she finds her hat and puts it on. She answers the
phone.

MERCEDES. Hello? *(Pause)* Who the fuck are you? OK so you know
my name. Big deal. What gives you the right to call me up at this time
of night, the hour of the fucking wolf? *(Pause)* I would dispute that
there was any emotion transference going on in this conversation
whatsoever. I'm just angry with you that's all. Of course I can be
angry with a stranger. No, I'm not afraid of myself. Well is that so.
I can tell you that the people who know me well are **terrified**. My
psychiatrist, after he's had a session with me, he has to have two
rest cures and a holiday! Don't get all sympathetic now. I eat sympathetic people for breakfast. What d'you want to know? Well
you must want something off of me, otherwise why phone?
You can't get out of the refrigerator? Tough. Call the fire brigade.
You can't get out of my refrigerator? Well what the fuck are you
doing there in the first place? *(Phone down, gets up still with hat on*
and opens fridge. White light floods out. As she does this a figure
appears behind her.) Mother? *(She shuts the fridge door, and she and*
the mother figure, which will be played by ROGER; *sit on the*
settee. ROGER *tilts his head modestly.)* Don't look at me like
that. In the end nobody ate—you weren't . . . eaten. If that's
what you came about. I'm right off food. *(Pause)* Why are you
dressed like that, as if you've been to some famous whore's
funeral . . . *(The* MOTHER *looks down again modestly and*
begins to pare the fingernails with a lemon stick.) I wish you wouldn'
do that while I'm talking to you. Mother. Are you listening?
Mother I'm in the middle of a battle for my sanity. Someone else
has got it at the moment. Not me. And if I knew where it was I am so
mad, so desperate that to get to it, to survive the next ten minutes, I
would tear them apart with my bare hands. Simply in order to survive

D'you understand that? D'you see that you too may have a part to
play in this? That your hands may not be entirely clean . . . That
cleanliness may not be next to godliness? You don't help. You're
not helping in this at all. And if I don't have it out with you, it's
not just going to be a fight to the death, is it now? It's not the way
to bless people and make them whole by telling them that they have
a sick spirit. I dream of my father. He complains about food. If we
ever—if we once—had had one conversation that was about a truth
that wasn't food . . . I bet you preferred me to be fat. I meant you
hadn't let me go. I want you to let me go, now. And I don't want
you ever coming back, hanging around here. I'll tell you why. I'm
not dippy except to the extent that I swallow your life and times
and carry it around in me like a dead calf. Of course I get sick.
And—mad—but mad at you. Are you going to let me go? Or am
I going to have to kill you all over again? *(MOTHER puts away the
lemon stick and stands.)* Don't go. You ambiguous woman. *(The
MOTHER snickers briefly, behind her hand.)* Don't laugh at what
you don't understand! You don't have natural understanding. You
buried it away. Do you understand why you have to let me go?
(MOTHER watchful.) I have a dream, which you will not understand. I'm in a white room, and they're testing me, to be a doctor.
And they fail me; not because I don't have an adequate bedside
manner or I have dirty hands, but because I am crazy. They can
see the crack as clearly as if I had a hare lip. Right there, in the
corner of my fingernail, they can see where I've bitten off a bit
too much skin—the blood. They can see I want to make a film of
Jesus Christ. They say, the state has decided that there was no
such figure as Jesus Christ, so it is even less likely that he was a
woman. So you have less than no chance of making it. In fact you've
got to go out, and unmake it every day of your life. I say, I can't do
that, I don't know what you mean. *(Figure of the MOTHER turns
and begins to exit. Stately, matronly. Noise of rising wind.
MERCEDES shouts after.)* I don't know what you mean! I don't
know what you mean! *(MOTHER exits gracefully. MERCEDES
reaches for the phone.)* Where's the Delphic oracle—Doctor Robert?
I just had a visit from the unconscious—at least I think it was—
Doctor Robert—can you just check this out with me—are my parents
dead? *(Pause. Question.)* I never talked about them to you? My
shrink? Well didn't you ever think to ask? Doctor Robert, what's
your first name? I've always wanted to ask. I know you've got a rule
about your distance from patients but—Andrew? That's a nice name.
Well, Andy, you're fired. *(Phone down. Pause. She's disconsolate.)*
If I could drag it out of me . . . on my own. No *(Pulling at her stomach.)*
Oh come on come on . . . What a **dog** . . . black dog black animal sitting,
in the dark, waiting. *(The stage grows darker.)*
IRENE'S VOICE. Help me.

A low spotlight on IRENE *in the doorway. She's wearing a hospital shift but it only reaches as far as her hips. Her legs are covered with blood. She reaches out her hands.*

MERCEDES. Come right on it.

IRENE *(whishper).* I'm tired.

Spot on another figure beside her. It's ROGER. *He's got his jacket on, but not trousers. He wears a belt on the outside. He carries a trident and net like a gladiator. Militant.*
He prods IRENE *with the trident. She does not react.*
Prods her again. She strains forward but is held from behind by something
He raises the trident a third time but does not strike.
IRENE *offers a great shriek and takes one small step forward, straining.*
ROGER *follows her, tabloid, with his trident raised but does not strike again. Gradually drops his pose.*
Build in music and general light.
Music: 'Behold the Lamb of God'.
ROGER *speaks over the opening chords.*

ROGER *(demotic).* Bethlehem! Out doors! Cold!
   Unfinished business during old winter's song.
   Bugger the snow at the start of the lambing season.
   Outside the town, all police leave cancelled—
   A bleeding convoy. Never realised
   Parthenogenesis was so fucken' 'ard.
   The bright star might as well have been a fridge
   For all the bleeding heat it gave to me.
   Why couldn't she done it in the proper place?

Music swells.
IRENE *is making progress towards the table but slowly. Every step she shrieks, piercingly.*
As she traverses the stage, we see what is holding her back: an umbilicus like cord stretches from the doorway, taut.
ROGER *fends off imaginary onlookers fiercely to clear her route.*

ROGER. Move along sir. Out the road.

The music climaxes.
IRENE *makes it to the table and falls on to it. The cord slackens a little.*
IRENE *collapses.*
The music dies away.
ROGER *gets out a knife and cuts through the umbilicus behind her.*

ROGER. Pity you couldn't have waited, Mary. Only a few hundred
   yards short of the manager an' all.

IRENE *(breathless).* I'm not Mary. I'm her mother.

ROGER. You're **not** . . . ? Oh dear. I mean, I've got a job to do—
   *(*IRENE *shakes her head.)* Excuse me, love, but where is she then?

(IRENE points off down the slack umbilicus.) Still pregnant?

IRENE. Yes.

ROGER. Thank god for small mercies. *(Pause)* C'mon c'mon we got to get her into that manger before she has it right here in the street. You! *(Pointing to* MERCEDES*)* And you! *(To* IRENE*)* Get on that rope!

Handel's stately music strikes up again at the beginning as they organise themselves into a tug-of-war team. MERCEDES *becomes the anchorman, with* IRENE *and* ROGER *pulling in front of her. They pull easily at first till they get into position the dowstage side of the table. The rope stretches out of the partition door. They pull strenuously. Sometimes they lose ground but mainly gain. Through the music is heard the loud braying of a donkey. The joint effort slackens as* IRENE *collapses from exhaustion. Music fades.*

ROGER. C'mon get up! C'mon! *(He prods her with the trident unavailingly.)*

IRENE. You've got to give me something . . . Pethedin . . . Or I can't . . . *(She starts to crawl away but* ROGER *nets her and prods her viciously.)*

ROGER *(turns to* MERCEDES*)*. You'd think it was you giving birth now wouldn't you the way she goes on. *(*IRENE *seizes the moment to make good her escape.* ROGER *exits after her.)* Oi! You! Back in line!

Music starts up again at beginning.
MERCEDES *takes up the rope and pulls. Titanic effort.*
Slowly inch by inch something is seen to be parting the office partition. What comes through is a platform tableau of MARY *and* JOSEPH *and the donkey, slightly oversize in the case of the humans. The donkey is a spotted inflatable horse as used by swimmers. It is reluctant to go forward.*

MARY *and* JOSEPH *are very similar. They have big noses and jaws and dopey expressions. They are made out of sacking and coarse material. Their eyes are set close together. Their mouths can move to speak. They are both grotesquely fat in the stomach: pregnant.*
They advance on the trolley as MERCEDES *reels in the umbilical rope. The music stops again as the donkey deflates with a sigh and falls down dead.*

MARY *and* JOSEPH *speak to each other—slow, dopey voices, lisping, earnest, low, booming.*

JOSEPH. Mary . . . I think we've got a problem with the donkey.

MARY. Looks alright to me.

JOSEPH. No, it's not having a rest this time, I think they've blown the last whistle on this animal. Poor creature.

MARY. They're expecting us on a donkey.

89

JOSEPH. Not all the way. We can't push it any further. It smelt bad
   enough when it was alive, god knows what it's going to be like when
   it's dead. I was sold a pup, face it. Anyhow, don't want to go to
   Bethlehem. What are they going to say when they find out we're
   both pregnant? Oh! Look over there. *(Points to* MERCEDES.)
MARY. Little girl—could we borrow your table? I'm Mary. This is my
   husband Joseph, and we're both about to give birth.
JOSEPH. It sounds strange, I know, but I really am her husband, and
   I really am . . . pregnant. How come, eh? I suppose that's what you're
   thinking. How come. Mary can explain it better than I can.
MARY. Well . . . Joseph was always interested in **girls**.
JOSEPH. Hee heee hee.
MARY. But didn't get engaged until very late in life.
JOSEPH. So no-one knew about—
MARY. No-one knew about his **outworks**.
JOSEPH. Except for a close circle of friends of course.
MARY. It seemed quite normal for him to be brought up as a boy . . .
JOSPEH. I just got engaged to Mary, and we'd hardly even held hands,
   when we went for a walk and—**Boum!** The lightning struck.
MARY. The lightning struck.
JOSEPH. And gorblimey we found we was **both** pregnant. So can we
   please have them here on the table. *(Pause)*
MERCEDES. Normally I'd say yes. But I have this problem. You see,
   this isn't my office any more. I have decided to leave. I have decided
   to leave.
JOSEPH *(a disappointed sneer)*. Oh, back to the drawing board . . . .

*The music strikes up again and they inch out in reverse, a little quicker
than they came in.*
MERCEDES *coils up the rope and slings it over the deflated donkey.*

MARY. Drawing board? What drawing board? *(Exiting)* I think they shoul
   get the goddamned drawing board to look at your outworks for a start

Exeunt tableau. The partition closes. Lights back to normal.
MERCEDES *pushes off the fridge through the main door. Returns to her
chair and waits.*
A lock turns in the door. ROGER *enters. He has a fur coat which he take.
off and hangs up. He has a briefcase.*
He turns and sees MERCEDES.

ROGER. I asked the janitor to keep you out of here at night. I asked hi
   call the police. *(Pause)* How long have you been here? Have you been l
   all night? How did you get in? You don't work here any more Miss Mc
   I want you to leave right away. *(Pause)* Even through the window wou
   be fast enough.
MERCEDES. Sure. D'you think I'm crazy enough to stay where I'm not
   wanted? Do you think I'm crazy?
ROGER. There's a short description of psychiatry, which is quite accura

its bottom line, it's conversation. And I don't want to talk to you.
(Pause)

MERCEDES. You're right I should be going. But I have this fear of
heights. I don't want to pass too near the window.

ROGER. Would you like me to close the blind for you? *(Pause)*

MERCEDES. No. *(Pause)* I don't like you enough. *(*ROGER *closes
the blind.)* Don't tell me, there must be another reason why you
did that. You're having a script conference in here, and you don't want
the window to be bugged by laser from that new condominium
opposite. Am I right?

ROGER. You are crazy.

MERCEDES. You ripped off my idea.

ROGER. I registered the idea. In my name.

MERCEDES. Please, I'm not going to argue with you.

ROGER. I can't take you back, even if you cured yourself overnight
in here. I've given your job to someone else. *(*MERCEDES *nods
sagely.)* I think you should take the hint when it's as broad as
being fired.

MERCEDES. Sure.

ROGER. I'm going to get the janitor to throw you out. Now

ROGER *exits.*

Pause.

IRENE *comes in dressed as at the beginning. She takes off her fur coat.*

IRENE. Where should I put this?

MERCEDES. I don't know where they hang coats in this place. I
never had one. *(Pause)* There. *(Points to* ROGER'S *coat.* IRENE
hangs hers up.)

IRENE. So this is Roger's? It's nice.

MERCEDES. He'll have yours, if he prefers it.

IRENE. I rather gather you didn't hit it off together. I'm sorry.

MERCEDES. Let's keep the sorrow within reasonable bounds. It's got
nothing to do with you.

IRENE. What will you do?

MERCEDES. I'll get by. I can give up my apartment and go and stay
with my mother. We get on pretty well. But I'll be around for the
rest of the week. Would you like to go out for a meal maybe before
I go?

IRENE. I think I'm going to be pretty busy here.

MERCEDES. I could tell you my side of the story.

IRENE. Thank you. Yes. That would be nice.

MERCEDES. I'll give you a call.

IRENE. I wish you well.

MERCEDES *takes* ROGER'S *fur coat and puts it on and preens a little.
She crosses to* IRENE *and kisses her lightly on the cheek.*
ROGER *comes back in as* MERCEDES *is going out.*

MERCEDES. Byeeee!

ROGER *looks at her disbelievingly. He can't actually believe she's decided to g*
MERCEDES, *full of a sudden jollity, waves to him as she closes the door.*
Too late, ROGER *realizes that she's taken his coat. He remains frozen for a se*
his pleasure at seeing MERCEDES *finally gone struggling with his desire not to*
let his fur coat go.
We never see the resolution of the conflict. MERCEDES *has left the room and*
launched herself on an uncertain future, and that is, has to be, the end of the p